MW00714704

THAT'S MY STORY - BOOK 1

Taking a Courageous Path

A search for who I am and the spiritual growth that just happened along that journey.

Estelle R. Reder

Eloquent Books
New York, New York

Eloquent Books
An imprint of AEG Publishing Group
845 Third Avenue, 6th Floor - 6016
New York, NY 10022
www.eloquentbooks.com

ISBN 978-1-60860-253-7

Printed in the United States of America

Book Design: Linda W. Rigsbee

TABLE OF CONTENTS

Dedication

To my wonderful son Marc and my beautiful daughter-in-law Lizanne, to my fantastic grandsons Mathew and Christopher - who have, through their love, given me reality, feedback, and truth.

This book would not have been written, had it not been for my Reiki Master/Teacher, Cheryl Whitebone, who saw it in a vision and said that I had a story to tell.

There have been many who assisted me on this journey. I give thanks to my sister Monique Piette, who has been my staunchest supporter, as well as Suzanne Zonneveld, Sue Lagasse, Karen Lefebvre, Kathy Hammond, Maureen Morris and Leslie Wellman, who have been there for me during many phases of my life. To my extraordinary friend, Melody Jones, who introduced me to my spirit guides, and to Fieronan, my "fierce warrior" guardian angel.

To my beloved parents, Raymond and Olive Peloquin, who believed in me and lovingly supported me in good times and tougher times and who gave my siblings and me the gifts of life, laughter, and love.

To my friend and Yoga teacher, Candace Csordas, who helped me to remember the breath of life and to remember what needed to be said in this book through our many private conversations. To my fellow Reiki Masters and friends Lori Mondor and Romalda Wildeman for their laughter, their healing energy, and their constant loving energy.

To my friend, Gwen Schentag, who, as a writer herself, helped me with the intricacies of the book set-up and preparing this book for publication.

To my editor and friend Marianne Gillis, for her countless hours of dedication to editing that ensured the success of the final product.

To my psychic Erika in Edmonton, my spiritual intuitive Margaret in Winnipeg, and to Kim McDonald who channels Babaji...for their incredible abilities to see and guide one's journey, without prejudice or judgment, but in light and love.

One of my favorite writers, Thich Nhat Hanh, states, "As we cultivate peace and happiness in ourselves, we also nourish peace and happiness in those we love." The more we can love and appreciate others, the more energy flows into us.

I want to acknowledge all of you – dear friends, colleagues, and teachers (whether two-legged, four-legged, or winged) – who have nourished my own peace and happiness. You have all helped me through my life's journey leading up to this book. I want to thank as well, all the people who consented to have their names and stories included.

To all my Masters and Spirit Guides, for the many insights and wisdom they have imparted, as well as every kindred spirit who has come into my life.

I am appreciative for all that you have taught me.

Thank You!

Introduction

We are capable of so much simply as human beings. We have extraordinary abilities yet to be explored. We are just beginning to conceive of the possibilities that this reality has to offer.

The ancients have always understood energy, how to transform it and use it to heal and enlighten. While studying to become a Reiki Master, I was told by my Reiki Master and Teacher, Cheryl Whitebone, that a story inhabited me. This story needed to be told and, that through this process, others would also be healed, as they related it to their own story.

"But what am I to write about?" I asked.

Cheryl Whitebone replied, "There is a story living inside of you, lurking around you. It will make its home within you very soon." Her voice was strong but held a quiet force like her eyes. Her tone was kind, yet she seemed never to say anything to me that did not have special meaning.

"Everyone has their own story to tell. Each story involves happiness, pain, joy, injustice, successes, romantic upsets, emotional hits, and wonderful experiences that they have lived over the years. It is the yin and yang of life. It's the ups and downs. It's our special story," she added.

"You have gained knowledge, through your life experiences, but that knowledge is wasted and is of no use to you until you share it with others," she continued.

Pain is nature's way of telling us that something in us needs to be healed, so let's get on with the healing. I want to share with you some of the experiences that I went through, how I was able to learn to let go of the hurts and how to have enough faith and trust to let self come into the next part of life.

One needs to work through the various levels of healing, each at their own pace. It is important to give this period the time it needs, to awaken parts of the self that have been paralyzed, repressed or unknown. However, it is only when you see life at its darkest moments that you tap into your inner strength, that you find your courage and that you realize all life is hope.

After a major change like divorce, one needs time to mourn what was crushed. One needs time to let it sink in that the anticipated dreamed-of future will not come to pass but that new hope comes with new beginnings.

Only the self, I think, can name (and free) those demons – friendly or otherwise – that keep us from being the kind of person we would like to be.

Over the years, I have written down faithfully the extraordinary events that have taken place in my life. I am more and more concerned with truth and so I have tried to be true to what I learned and to record the memories clearly of the events that changed my life and the powerful women who helped me with that transformation. This is a true story. Some of the names and the places in this book have been changed to protect the privacy of those involved.

A search for who I am, and the spiritual growth that "just happened" along that journey is my story. It is the story of a woman unraveling the mysteries of selfhood. It is my personal journey.

This book is that story.

PART I

Time for Change

(1995)

LEAVING

Some of us were leaving
little towns and pretty places
though we thought them ugly at the time.

That is not to say
that we were special
set apart from those who stayed.
We were movers
but of our own selves only.

Not unlike the cabbage
grown for city market
there came a time to be detached
and trucked away.

And we went willingly.

Rod McKuen

CHAPTER 1

The Decision

1995

I stood looking out the kitchen window, watching as the sun rose slowly in the East, over the serene Canadian landscape, in small-town St. Adolphe, Manitoba. The early morning wind was bending the grass and trees in the flat wheat fields across the street where we lived. It was early August and the wheat was ripening to a gold color. Soon, the harvest would begin again.

I pulled my eyes away from the spectacular rising sun and returned to where I was sitting at the kitchen table. It was my first day of a month's holiday. My husband and I had not planned any major trips this year. We thought we would just enjoy golfing at courses around the province, and enjoy our home.

We had a big property and I was looking forward to expanding some of the flowerbeds and making other improvements around the yard and house. I had my plant book and a scale drawing of the garden, planning changes for next year, as I sat at the table having my morning coffee.

My husband John walked into the kitchen and said, "Now what are you doing?" I replied, "I'm just looking at flowers and how to plant things differently for next year."

"I suppose you're just going to plant things without checking with me, just like you did with that plant you just bought for the front yard. You never even asked me before planting it there," he exclaimed indignantly.

I looked up with a surprised look on my face. "That bothered you?" I asked. "Well, yes, we both live here," he replied.

I patiently put my book down and said, "Well, John, it was a five dollar plant. If you don't like it there, just move it to where you think it should go. It's not a big deal!"

"Yes, it is a big deal," he retorted angrily. "You're always doing stuff like that, without consulting me."

I slowly closed my books on the table, got up and said, "I'm going for a long walk," leaving through the back door. While walking, the thoughts that I had pushed back in my mind for at least seven years, kept coming back to me: "Estelle, you have got to get out of this relationship…you're dying here".

"It's getting worse, instead of better," I reflected as I walked. A few weeks earlier, my house cleaner had advised me that she was moving away. I sat down with John and mentioned that, until I could find a replacement, he would have to help me with the cleaning.

All he was required to do was the heavy vacuuming in the bedroom, down two sets of stairs, and the family room on the lower level, which was hardly ever used anymore.

He looked at me pensively, and said, "Well, I'll think about it." I really thought he was joking, so I just let it go, and went on about the day. The next morning, at breakfast, he started the conversation: "I've thought about it, and the answer is no!"

I had forgotten what we were talking about, so totally puzzled, asked, "What was the question?"

"You asked me to do the heavy vacuuming, and the answer is no, I don't want to do it."

I looked at him with incredulity: "What? You won't do it. Why not?"

"Because I don't want to," he replied.

"Well, John," I answered reasonably, "it's only temporarily, until I get a replacement cleaning lady. You know that when I do the vacuuming, my back[1] goes out, and I'm in pain for two to three days, have to go to the chiropractor, and take painkillers; otherwise, I'd do it myself."

"I know," he countered, "and I still don't want to do it."

So I recapped, "OK, let me get this straight. You do not do any housework, no cooking, laundry, ironing, and dusting…not any household work whatsoever. You do the groceries once a week on Saturday mornings and you cut the grass in summer, clear the snow in winter."

"I've never asked for your help doing the housework," I continued, "even while raising our son Marc, and holding a full-

---

[1] See Emotional Source of Disease, on page …. For back pain, the emotional source is not feeling supported emotionally, needing support.

time job. I'm asking now, this simple temporary request, and your answer is no?" I recapped in disbelief: "even knowing that when I do the vacuuming, that I'm in terrible pain for the next few days, you're okay with that?" I asked again.

"That's right," he said, and marched out to the garage to work on one of his woodworking hobbies.

So, as I'm walking and reflecting on that conversation, and the one this morning about the plant position, it hits me like never before, "There's nothing left of this marriage…no love, no hate, no frustrations, no fears. I feel nothing. I am empty."

"It's over," I tell myself, "this time, it's really over. I have to get out of here before I die." The thoughts circle in my head. Twenty-eight years. How many of those years did I wish away, not wanting to be "here"?

I think back to how John and I met. I had moved to Winnipeg from St. Malo, after completing Grade 11 at the local high school.

I decided to take Secretarial Science, a two-year program at Red River Community College instead of completing Grade 12. I was 17 years old when I left home.

My brother Noel and his wife Annette were living in St. Boniface. They very kindly offered to give me room and board while I went to College. They were very good to me during the 14 months it took me to complete the program at accelerated speed.

I got my first job as Secretary for the Appraisal Institute of Canada. My starting salary was eighty-two dollars per month. I was thrilled to pieces. I moved out of my brother's place, and moved in with my girlfriend Ev Catellier. We had been friends throughout our childhood, and lived only three houses apart.

She had also moved to the city at the same time and lived in a rooming house on the same street as my brother, so we hung out together when I was not studying.

We were so happy to be sharing a very small apartment that we could both afford. How small was it? It was so small that we had a couch that opened up as a bed that doubled as our kitchen. Pretty small, but we did not care. We were two independent 18 year olds on our own and the world was our oyster.

While I was going to the College, I had to take three buses to get there. After a while, I noticed there was a man who was taking the exact same buses at the same bus stop and getting off at the College. We started talking on the bus trips. His name was Don Hodgson. He had moved to Winnipeg from Saskatchewan and I really liked him. We became good friends. I thought that Ev and Don might like each other, so I introduced them and they started dating. About a year later, they decided to move to Edmonton, as Don got a job there. I was sad to see them go. Therefore, I lost my friend and my roommate…now, what was I to do?

While taking another bus downtown, I met up with Pauline and Jocelyn Carriere, from St-Pierre, a neighboring town. It turns out, they were looking for another place to live, and I told them so was I. We decided to move in together, the three of us, and found a great spacious apartment, The Gaboury Apartments, right across from the Police Station in St-Boniface.

We had great neighbors…a bunch of single police officers living below us, a married police officer, and his wife living next door to us. We felt safe there, and we got along pretty good, overall. The next-door neighbor was helping coach a woman's fastball team, the St. Vital Comettes. He suggested that I try out for the team and so I did, and I made the cut.

Thereafter, I was playing baseball twice a week and playing fastball tournaments on weekends. It was a great time. I was dating different people, just could not seem to find "the one," and so kept dating casually.

My boyfriend, Noel Joyal, had dumped me a few months earlier and I was having a hard time getting over it and moving on. After all, this was the man I was sure I was going to marry. I had loved him with all my heart and soul. I poured all my energy into playing baseball and hanging out with the team, dating casually and just getting into my own adulthood.

One night, at baseball practice, I heard a car honking behind the fence and when I turned around saw this person in a yellow convertible talking to a group of girls who were hanging onto his car. A car had driven up behind him and, as he was blocking the entire road, he had honked his car after waiting for the yellow convertible to move, which he had not. He honked his horn again. Again, the yellow convertible did not move. He honked his horn a third time and as I was watching, the yellow convertible put his car into reverse and gunned the motor, and smashed into the car that was honking, trying to get around him.

The man in the other car came out scratching his head: "What did you do that for? I was only trying to get around you." With a smirk on his face, he turned to the girls and said, "Girls…you saw it all, didn't you? He smashed into me, didn't he?" The girls all giggled and nodded "Yes."

The poor man looked around in bewilderment. I yelled out to him, "Hey mister, I saw the whole thing. If you want a witness, come and see me. He deliberately smashed into your car." He was so relieved and the person in the yellow convertible looked at me with a scowl on his face, shrugged his shoulders, and took off.

That was such a bizarre incident that I had just witnessed. It turns out that I was the only one who had seen the entire thing take place, other than the girls who all ran off as soon as the yellow convertible left.

The man came over and talked to me and we were both shaking our heads in disbelief that someone would deliberately do something like that. I gave him my work phone number, in case he ever did need me as a witness. Up to that point, I had been pretty naïve about the city and was casual about walking around by myself at night. I had not "seen" the dangers around a big city. This small incident really opened my eyes that all you see is not always as it seems.

Obviously, this driver of the yellow convertible had a mean streak or an uncontrollable temper, or a very large ego, and so, even if he was good looking, this was no reason to trust him, based only on appearances.

Another bizarre incident happened during a baseball game to Shirley, one of our team members. She was our catcher. It was a very hot summer night and, during the game, she just keeled over and passed out. Then she started shaking and rolling around. Everybody was freaking out except me. I recognized immediately that she was having an epileptic episode.

I recognized the symptoms because one of my classmates in St. Malo had also been epileptic. After the first seizure there, where everybody tried to hold him down and someone put a spoon in his mouth to prevent him from swallowing his tongue (which is a fallacy and only caused him a lot of damage and pain to his mouth). Anyways, his mother came to the school and told us not to be scared but, that if it happened again, just to remove anything around him that could be harmful. Then, just let him be. Watch to make sure he is still breathing and, if necessary, turn him on his side, but not to restrain him in any way. The epileptic seizure only lasts a minute or so, and then they come around on their own. To try to restrain them in any way only causes them pain after. I have never forgotten that information afterwards.

This came in handy when Shirley fell over and started having an epileptic seizure. I just told everyone to stand back, removed any equipment that was in the area, and just let her be. When she came around, she was disoriented. She did not know who she was or where she was.

At that point, I told some team members to call an ambulance and they were able to contact her parents. I drove with her in the ambulance and held her hand. I stayed with her until her parents came. They informed me that it had been unnecessary to call the ambulance and to call them directly if ever it happened again. They would come and pick her up. They reassured me that it often takes up to 30 minutes before the brain kicks in fully and they remember who and where they are. Simply let them lie or sit quietly until they recover completely. Usually, they need to sleep for a few hours afterwards, as the epilepsy takes its toll on the body.

At the next practice, when Shirley came over to the baseball diamond, she could not look anyone in the eye. She was embarrassed and everyone else was uncomfortable. So, I walked up to her, gave her a hug, and said: "Hey girl...next time you're going to keel over like that, can you wait until it's the third out?" We all laughed, that broke the ice and play resumed.

She sheepishly said that she should have told someone of her condition, in case it ever happened, but she was too ashamed. We all hugged her and told her: "Hey, it's a medical condition. There is no shame in that. Just warn us next time." I made her promise she would alert someone at work as well.

She told us that her parents were quite financially compromised and that they had no insurance. The ambulance bill had been $120. So, if it ever happens again, she asked us not to call the ambulance, simply call her parents or let her sit quietly, even if it takes an hour. We all agreed to deal with it that way, if ever it happened again. The next week, I asked all members of the baseball team to pitch in to help pay this bill, which we did.

I researched epilepsy and found out that Epilepsy is a common chronic neurological disorder characterized by recurrent unprovoked seizures. These seizures are transient signs and/or symptoms due to abnormal or excessive neuronal activity in the brain. About 50 million people worldwide have epilepsy at any one time. Epilepsy is usually controlled, but not cured, with medication. Not all epilepsy syndromes are life-long – some forms are confined to particular stages of childhood. Epilepsy involves episodic abnormal electrical activity in the brain.

In most cases, the proper emergency response to a generalized epileptic seizure is simply to prevent the patient from self-injury by moving him or her away from sharp edges, placing something soft beneath the head, and carefully rolling the person into the recovery position to avoid asphyxiation.

In some cases the person may seem to start snoring loudly following a seizure, before coming to. This merely indicates that the person is beginning to breathe properly and does not mean he or she is suffocating. Should the person regurgitate, the material should be allowed to drip out the side of the person's mouth by itself. If a seizure lasts longer than five minutes, or if the seizures begin coming in "waves" one after the other – then Emergency Medical Services should be contacted immediately. Prolonged seizures may develop into a dangerous condition requiring hospitalization and emergency treatment.

Objects should never be placed in a person's mouth by anybody – including paramedics – during a seizure as this could result in serious injury to either party. Despite common folklore, it is not possible for a person to swallow their own tongue during a seizure. However, it is possible that the person will bite their own tongue, especially if an object is placed in the mouth.

With other types of seizures such as simple partial seizures and complex partial seizures where the person is not convulsing but may be hallucinating, disoriented, distressed, or unconscious, the person should be reassured, gently guided away from danger, and sometimes it may be necessary to protect the person from self-injury, but physical force should be used only as a last resort as this could distress the person even more. In complex partial seizures wherethe person is unconscious, attempts to rouse the person should not be made as the seizure must take its full course. After a seizure, the person may pass into a Deep sleep or otherwise they will be disoriented and often unaware that they have just had a seizure, as amnesia is common with complex partial seizures. The person should remain observed until they have completely recovered.

After a seizure, it is typical for a person to be exhausted and confused. Often The person is not immediately aware that they have just had a seizure. During this time, one should stay with the person - reassuring and comforting them – until they appear to act as they normally would. Seldom during seizures do people lose bladder or bowel control, but it can happen. In some instances the person may vomit after coming to. People should not eat or drink until they have returned to their normal level of awareness, and they should not be allowed to wander about unsupervised. Many patients will sleep deeply for a few hours after a seizure – this is common for those having just experienced a more violent type of seizure. Headaches may occur after a seizure. These headaches share many features with migraines, and respond to the same medications.

It is helpful if those present at the time of a seizure make note of how long and how severe the seizure was. It is also helpful to note any mannerisms displayed during the seizure. For example, the individual may twist the body to the right or left, may blink, might mumble nonsense words, or might pull at clothing. Any observed behaviours, when relayed to a neurologist, may be of help in diagnosing the type of seizure which occurred.

Years later, after I became Manager, one afternoon, there was only myself and one of my secretaries in the office. All of a sudden, I heard a deep moan and a thump. When I rushed over to her desk, she was lying on the floor and starting to shake and going into an epileptic episode. Because I had already gone through it twice before, I knew what to do. I made sure nothing around could hurt her and I just let her get through it on her own.

One of the worst things about someone going through an epileptic episode is that they have no control over their bodily functions, and so will often wet themselves, which is the most embarrassing thing for them to face once they come out of it.

I quickly ran to the bathroom, grabbed a bunch of paper towels and, once she came to, gave them to her to help dry her off as much as possible. She apologized profusely and turned red with shame. I told her: "Hey, there is nothing to be apologetic about. I've dealt with this condition twice before with other people it happened to, and so...just sit here quietly and I'll call your husband."

She said: "Well, my husband is out of town on business. Please call my parents and they will come to get me." I would have paid a taxicab to take her home, but I didn't want to leave her alone once she got there. I couldn't drive her myself, as I was holding down the fort, being the only person in the office with appointments coming in all afternoon.

Fortunately, this happened in between appointments and I was the only "witness" to the incident. She was very grateful for that. I immediately called maintenance and explained that there had been a "chemical spill" on the carpet, and requested that someone come immediately to ensure that it didn't stain or leave any smell. They took care of it.

The next year, when baseball season rolled around, our coach got us all together at spring try-out, as we had some new players who had joined the team. After the try-out, four of his friends came over to talk with us. He introduced us to Bob Lang, Peter Funk, John Penner, and Ben Sawatzky. He warned us that the first two were married, and last two were single. I thought that he had pointed out John Penner as one of the married ones and was quite disappointed when he accepted becoming assistant coach.

John would pick me up first and then we would pick up four other girls in the neighbourhood to go play at tournaments, as none of us had cars at the time. I would always sit in the back seat, even though I was the first one he picked up. I really liked him, but hey…he was married (or so I thought at the time)…so "hands-off".

One night, I suggested that he take his wife to see the new movie: "The Sound of Music." He replied, "My wife? I'm not married." I answered: "But I thought our coach said you were married when we were introduced at the start of the baseball season."

"Nope, you got it wrong. It's Pete and Bob who are married. Ben and I are the single ones," he confirmed.

"Really," I replied casually. On the next pick-up, I sat in the front seat and we started dating shortly thereafter.

We decided to get married the next spring and chose April 8, 1967 as it was the only day the church and hall were available. I entered into that marriage with such love, faith and hope that we would have as great a marriage as my own parents, my role models.

As custom would dictate, I did not see John until I walked into the church and saw him standing at the altar, waiting for me. As soon as I got up to him, I could see that he had been drinking, probably all night long, and was still "under the influence". I was shocked. That was my first twinge of unease, but I shrugged it off and went through with the wedding.

Well, married life wasn't what I had imagined it to be. We were both working all day, and then I would come home and do all the

"women" things, like cook, clean, wash, iron, food shopping, decorating the house that we were renting on St. Mary's Road.

John wouldn't even help clean up, wash or dry the dishes "in case one of my friends would come in and catch me helping you." Hmmm…okay, I wasn't impressed but I was young (20) and he was supposedly a mature twenty-six-year-old. I thought it would change but it never did. If anything, he became more entrenched in his opinions as we grew apart.

Then, the most wonderful event happened in my life that I will thank John forever for. I became a mother. I had a son…Marc Robert Penner. He is the joy of my life, and I can never regret anything that I had to go through to have him in my life. From the moment that I felt his movements inside me, my life was forever changed. There was this fierce protectiveness in me and

 I knew I would give up my life for this new life growing in me.

From the moment I laid my eyes on him, it was instant and deep love, the love that wells up from deep inside you and makes your eyes water with gratitude for this unbelievable gift that God has bestowed upon you.

John was very jealous of Marc, of the attention that I gave him, and he continued his "week-end drinking binges", where he would go to the bar with his buddies Friday night after work, and he wouldn't come home until the wee hours of the morning. On Saturdays, he would leave for the pub around 11:00 a.m. and wouldn't return home until late Saturday night. Sundays, he would be nursing a hang-over and stay home with us, grouchy, miserable and finding all the negative things that he could to throw at me and us, as Marc got older.

I wanted to leave so many times, but I believed in our marriage vows and kept trying to make it work. We left, Marc and I, a few times, for a few days. He would find us, beg me to come back saying that he would quit drinking, that he would be a better husband and father. I believed him every time and would go back, only to have the same cycle start all over again after a few weeks.

He did love his sports, and so when he was involved in playing baseball or hockey or when he started coaching, he was better. Things got better for a number of years, as Marc grew up.

I wasn't able to get pregnant again, although I wanted another child so very much, but I realized that I would never be able to trust John ever. I knew I needed to make sure that I had a job and so, I focused on Marc and my career, so that if ever we left, I would be able to support the both of us.

I did get pregnant a few years later, but miscarried in the early months. The doctor suggested that I get my tubes tied, to ensure that I wouldn't have to go through that again. I had that done. From that moment on, I started focusing on making enough money to ensure that I would never have to worry about any man to look after me and Marc.

How swiftly time passes, I thought. Here it was, 28 years later, and I was telling myself: "It's over…this time, it's really over. I have to get out of here before I die." The thoughts circled in my head, as I walked around town that final decision-making day.

Then, I realized that, for the past two years, at least, every night, when I climbed into bed, I would turn away from my husband, and pray to God: "God…someone…anyone…rescue me from this nightmare I'm living."

Then I would make a pact with God: "Okay, God…one of us has to die, to get out of this situation. I don't care which one it is. I'll gladly die, right now, anytime…just to get out of here."

Dying was an easier out for me than leaving John and hurting him, his family, my family, and our friends. I don't handle confrontations very well on a personal level and John was a master at it.

So, generally, throughout our married life, I would usually back off, submerge my thoughts, my feelings, do whatever was needed to be done, just to keep peace in the house. It occurred to me that, in doing so, I had lost me somewhere along the way. I had become such an accomplished actress; no one had any idea what I was living through. Everyone thought we were happy and had an "ideal" marriage.

The sad part is that I was hurting myself the most by denying myself any real chance for true happiness. In the last six months, I kept having this recurring dream. There was this disjointed arm, which would travel up the stairs, like a snake, crawling along the floor to the edge of the bed, start to climb up on the bed, and as it got close to my face to grab me, I would wake up in a cold sweat. My heart would be pounding, and it would take me hours to get back to sleep. The next night…same dream. This continued for six months.

Later, I was to analyze this with Leslie, my friend, who is excellent at dream interpretations. She and I were discussing this one night, and when we looked it up in one of her dream interpretation books, there it was…under "disjointed arm"… Death or Divorce."[2]

The decision was made: "I'm finally leaving John," I firmly told myself, that fateful morning when I went on that long walk. The decision did not come easy, after 28 years of marriage, with

[2] Ball, Pamela. *10,000 Dreams Interpreted*, Arcturus Publishing Limited, 1966, "Death or Divorce. Also, Dismembered -can be taken in its literal sense – we are being torn apart. Sometimes this can suggest the need to restructure our lives and begin again. At other times, it can indicate that there is a way in which we are being threatened to the very core of our existence."

a Catholic background, aging parents, and our only child, Marc, now a husband of four years.

Although I felt that I would be letting everyone down, it had gotten to the point where it was down to my survival. It is surprising how that survival instinct kicks in when you least expect it.

I remembered good times (and there were good times) during our marriage. I also remembered all the times that I had wanted to leave, had left for short periods of time, but always, something had made me come back.

One incident, particularly, stood out in my mind. As our 25th anniversary had loomed, three years earlier, instead of looking at it as a wonderful milestone in our marriage, I thought to myself: "Estelle, another year has come and gone and you're still here. You should have been gone by now."

I did not want any celebration whatsoever; I felt like such a hypocrite…living this lie, while slowly dying inside, day after day. That had been three years ago and here I was –still prevaricating – but no more!

"This time, I'm really leaving for good." I firmly reiterated to myself as I walked home on that fateful day.

I had been seeing a chiropractor and massage therapist for the past twelve years, due mainly to a back injury from work from a partial wall falling on my spinal column at my neck. Ed Beaudry, my massage therapist, had been treating me, and knew where all the damage had been done and was helping me rebuild the damage to my upper back.

The week before, I had been there for my regular therapy session and as soon as he touched my back, I burst out crying. He never said anything, just kept on massaging the sore parts and after he left the room at the end of the session, he slipped a piece of paper under the door. When I bent over to pick it up, he had written: "Go for it!"

I kept that piece of paper with me, like a talisman, taking it out of my purse now and again, as if it would give me the courage and energy to do what I had to do to get out of there and make a life for myself. I didn't know what kind of life I wanted, but I now knew what kind of life I didn't want anymore.

THE BLISS OF SORROW

NEVER dry, never dry,
Tears that eternal love sheddeth!

How dreary, how dead doth the world still appear,
When only half-dried on the eye is the tear!

Never dry, never dry,
Tears that unhappy love sheddeth!

Johann Wolfgang von Goethe
1789

CHAPTER 2

The Leaving

As I walked back inside the house, I thought, "Okay, now that my mind has been made up - I've decided to leave -how I get the body out?" I knew that my husband would not take too well to this decision, so what was I to do?

I decided to move into the guest bedroom, so I moved some things in there throughout the day and when it came time to go to bed, I told my husband: "Oh, by the way, I'm going to be sleeping in the guest room, for the next little while. My back has been really bothering me, and perhaps sleeping alone, on a harder surface, will help improve it."

He said, "Sure," and gave me a strange look as he went upstairs to the master bedroom. The guest room was on the main floor and after I got into bed, I sat up facing the door. I knew that he was going to come back and that a major confrontation was coming up.

I asked God and my Guardian Angel to send help…to give me the strength and courage to face whatever would be coming up. Sure enough, less than a half an hour later, downstairs he came, and planted himself at the bedroom door, leaning on the door-jamb. "This isn't really about your back, is it?" he sneered at me.

And at that moment, something strange, but wonderful and magical, happened to me. I had my first out-of-body experience; I guess you would call it that.

As I sat there, leaning back against the pillows, what I can only describe as my soul, left my body and moved up into the far left corner of the room and I remember looking down at that woman on the bed, and hearing her say "that's right. It's not about my back."

From where I was looking down, I thought, "Wow, way to go, girl." I knew it was I, speaking those words, and yet I could stay detached and unafraid. At the time, there was so much happening that I had no time to analyze what was going on. I was just living it.

John marched into the guest room and sat down on the chair on the right side of the room, "So, do you want a divorce, then?" he asked, with a smile on his face. I heard myself say, "Yes, yes, I do!" From where I was observing, I thought, "She's actually said it. She's doing it."

Well, with a look of shock and surprise on his face, he said, "Let's talk about this, then."

I replied, "John, there's nothing left to talk about. We have talked for 28 years…you have talked for 28 years…I have listened. Anytime we had difficulties, you said you would change…that you would help me around the house; that you would cook one meal a week…and so on. Those things never materialized. It is too late for talk now. It's over! I'm leaving."

John talked, talked, and barraged me with arguments, insults. He hit me on all the emotional levels that he could. "How can you do that to your only son, if you really, really love him?" he countered. "What about your mom and dad? You know how devout Catholics they are. Have you no feelings for them?

"What about my mom? I thought you loved her?" he continued on and on, as I slowly, quietly started crying, and I kept crying throughout the verbal assault. I was still out-of-body, looking down at this woman who was crying and I felt such compassion for her.

He kept up the pressure for perhaps an hour; perhaps more…I lost track of time. Finally, he had run out of things to say and although I was crying, I had not once retaliated, or raised to the bait that he was casting out…I had not backed down or changed my decision.

He finally left the room, and as I came back down into myself, I was so surprised that my resolve had stayed strong. As I turned out the light, for an uneasy sleep -but I did sleep - I asked for strength and endurance, as I knew that the days ahead would not get any easier.

The next day, I went over to my girlfriend Sue Lagasse. We spent the afternoon lying around her swimming pool. I went on her air mattress, going around and around her pool, the action matching my thoughts that were going around and around in circles in my head. She left me alone, knowing there was a lot on my mind -

not knowing what, but she knew enough to leave me alone to figure it out on my own. I did this for two weeks solid.

In the meantime, the second day, John was going to a football game with our son, Marc. I asked him, "Are you going to tell Marc that I'm leaving?"

He replied, "Yes, I'll talk to him about it." I was surprised, as John had never really taken any initiative to talk with Marc about anything. At puberty, it was me that Marc came to…to find out about the "facts of life and stuff."

The next morning, John had gone out golfing, very early. Around 10:00 a.m., Marc phoned. I assumed that John had talked to him, as he had promised that he would. "So, Marc, how do you feel about what's happening?" I asked him immediately. He replied, "What's happening, mom?" I said, in shock, "You mean, your dad didn't tell you that I was leaving him?" I started to cry. Marc answered: "Mom…Lizanne and I are coming right over… are you going to be okay until we get there?" he asked, concerned. "Yes, I'll be okay." I answered, tearfully.

Half an hour later, Marc and Lizanne walked into the house, both hugged me, and we sat down to talk. They were both so supportive, and understanding. While I was trying to explain how I had come to this decision, at one point Marc said, "Mom, I lived here with you both. I remember how things were. Once especially, when I was about 12 years old, I said to my friend Sab, "Sab…mom and I are leaving dad. Another time," he continued, "was before Lizanne and I got married…four years ago…I was sure you were leaving with me, when I moved out that night."

Marc and I have always been close, and it came as no surprise that he had sensed the impending decision for a long time. "Mom," he whispered gently, as he held me tightly in his arms, "you have a right to be happy. You have to do what you want to do, for a change…not what everyone else thinks you should do."

Lizanne, my beautiful daughter-in-law, has been like a real daughter to me, from the moment I met her. Had I drawn up a blueprint of who I would like as a wife for my wonderful and only son, I would have drawn a picture of Lizanne.

We had become very close in the six years that I had known her.

She was so impressed that Marc, being an only child, knew how to cook, wash clothes, clean…, and listen! She remembered

the first date she had with Marc. He brought her home (while we were out), and cooked her a candlelight dinner… macaroni and cheese, with wieners and ketchup. I knew I could count on them, that morning, as we held each other in a circle of love and support.

THE ROSE FAMILY

The rose is a rose,
and was always a rose.

But the theory now goes
that the apple's a rose,

And the pear is, and so's
the plum, I suppose.

The dear only know
what will next prove a rose.

You, of course, are a rose—
But were always a rose.

Robert Frost

CHAPTER 3

Going Back in Time

The next day, I was back at work. Professionally, I was at the pinnacle of corporate success...for a woman. I had risen to the upper echelons of my career with the company I worked for since 1981.

My career had started out very humbly. I came from a big French family, living in the country, one hour's drive from the big city of Winnipeg, Manitoba (Canada), right smack in the middle of Canada and just across the border from North Dakota (U.S.A.). I was number seven, out of twelve children, and named Estelle Rose, after mom's sister...my godmother, Rose.

St. Malo, Manitoba (1964)

At seventeen years of age, I approached Mom and said, "Mom, I want to go to Red River Community College in Winnipeg." I did not know how I was going to be able to afford it, but I knew Mom would find a way...and she did.

On a Sunday afternoon, she called the Manager of the St. Malo Caisse Populaire and we walked over to his house. Mom explained to him that I wanted to go to school in Winnipeg, and that I would need a loan. After raising twelve children, Mom had started working at the local sewing factory. She did not make a lot of money but whatever she made helped.

Dad was a great carpenter and worked hard to make a decent home for us all but sometimes it just was not enough, so Mom had decided to go to work, in spite of protests from dad.

We were sitting at the kitchen table of the Manager's home when she said, "Dennis, my daughter wants to go to school in Winnipeg, and she's going to need money. How much do you think she would need for a year's stay in Winnipeg?" The Manager answered, "Well, let's see. Calculating her school fees, her room and board, and so on, $1,000.00 should be enough to see her through one year."

"Okay," Mom said. "I'll co-sign her loan." The Manager took out a loan application, Mom signed it, and we walked home, hand in hand. "Mom," I said humbly as I squeezed her hand, "you've given me a chance to make something of myself."

"I promise you this...that you'll never be stuck with any loan payment once I start to work and that I'll make you proud of me." I very seriously promised her. She squeezed my hand back and said, "I know that you will, otherwise we wouldn't be here right now."

"How are you going to tell Dad?" I asked worriedly. I knew that Dad would not be too thrilled with the idea that Mom had co-signed a big loan for me. (Hey, this was 1964, remember!... Mom was only making $12.00 per week, at the sewing factory, so $1,000.00 was a LOT of money, back then.)

Mom just smiled at me and said, "Leave your Dad to me. I'll make him understand why I had to do this." And I did...and she did. I do not know what was said between them but Dad came out to the living room and asked me, "Well, what it is exactly that you want to learn, with all that money?"

I had researched courses available at Red River Community College and wanted to go into Accounting. That course was all filled up for the year and I did not want to wait another year, so I signed up for the next best thing...Secretarial Science.

I learned how to type, and was actually the top of my class, at 130 words per minute...a skill that I have come to appreciate even more, especially when computers came into being! Some of you might remember "the Dictaphone." Well, I learned how to work that machine, and type correspondence from it.

As well, I learned "Pitman shorthand," a skill I use still today. When I am in meetings, and people are sitting close to me and I want to write things to do while have them thinking that I am listening, I do it in "Pitman Shorthand."

It intrigues people to see a bunch of squiggles. I invariably am nudged and asked, "What's that? What does that mean?" Then I explain some of the lines and strokes and what words they actually represent. It leaves people very impressed!

Therefore, I moved to the big city, boarded in with my oldest brother, Noel and his wife, Annette. They were expecting their first baby but very generously took me in. For a very nominal fee, they gave me room and board for over a year, while I studied very hard to complete my courses.

At that time, Secretarial Science was a two-year course but I only had money for one year. As you could go at your own pace, I worked doubly hard, and managed to get it done in fourteen months. I only had $10.00 left when I graduated and knew that I had to get a job, immediately! Therefore, I started going on job interviews.

One was especially funny! A friend of mine, Andy Chouinard, and I had been singing and playing guitar

together for the fun of it, for over a year. We had entered a few "coffee house-type" contests and won first prize. Therefore, we decided to enter the one on TV…a local talent contest. We did not win, but came in second. The following week, we entered the St. Boniface Music Festival, in 1964 and we were Awarded 1st Prize.

However, the Manager of the local Coca-Cola plant was watching that night and he told his assistant about it the next day. "They should have won that contest," he told her emphatically. Unbeknownst to him, his assistant was a friend of a friend of mine, who knew I was looking for a job. She phoned me and said, "Why don't you go down to see this guy. Maybe he'll give you a job."

Therefore, I phoned him, and explained who I was and got an interview. Well, it turned out he was more interested in my skills at singing and playing the guitar than he was in my secretarial skills. I didn't get the job! Nevertheless, it still makes me laugh when I think about it today.

After looking for work for a few weeks, I had $2.00 left when I found a job. It was humble beginnings, indeed. However, someone was willing to take a chance on me. It was as a secretary of the Appraisal Institute of Canada. I started at $82.00 a month. That was an incredible salary, especially for my first job.

I stayed there for a year and then got another job with a higher salary. After 17 years working with various levels of government, both Federal and Provincial, I decided it was time to join "private enterprise."

Mom and dad could not understand why I would leave such a secure position with the government to go and work for a big, bad private company. In addition, I was going to be working "out on the road." The first woman across Canada hired to work "out on the road," visiting accounts throughout the Province of Manitoba. There I was...twenty-two suits and me (that is how we referred to working with men). To quote Dickens: "It was the best of times...it was the worst of times."

I had had my first and only child (as it turned out) at the age of 20. This was 1967. Women were not expected to go back to work, once they had a baby. Therefore, working in the male-dominated financial world, it surprised me to encounter almost outright hostility from some men; once they found out I had a child.

Most suggested I should stay at home, care for my child, and leave the business to "them" (i.e. men). However, I patiently explained my situation to them, instead of reacting negatively. Most men surprisingly understood. I just worked doubly hard, and showed them that I knew what I was talking about…that I could be trusted and that I was not going away.

I find that if you are honest, straightforward, mean what you say and deliver what you promise, good things will happen…and they did. I had a few good men as mentors and they guided me through the minefields of the corporate world.

 There I was in 1995 and I was Regional Manager of Credit Union Insurance Services, Manitoba Region.

THE AFTER-ECHO

The mellow sounds that cliff and island gave,
Have lingered in the crescent bay,
Until, by lightest breezes fanned,
They float far off beyond the dying day
And leave it still as death.

But hark, —
Another singing breath
Comes from the edge of dark;
A note as clear and slow
As falls from some enchanted bell,
Or spirit, passing from the world below,
That whispers back, Farewell.
So in the heart,
When, fading slowly down the past,
Font memories depart,
And each that leaves it seems the last;
Lon g after all the rest are flown,
Returns a solitary tone, —
The after-echo of departed years, —
And touches all the soul to tears.

Henry Van Dyke

CHAPTER 4

Hope Rising

August 1995

Going home that night, I felt a glimmer of hope, that maybe I'd be able to do this, after all. My very survival was at stake, this I knew. I braced myself for the barrage that was to come, when I walked in the door that night. However, I was ill prepared for the weeks of continuous verbal pressure ahead of me.

At first, he was conciliatory and placating. He offered to move out, and leave me the house. I starred at him in disbelief. That was so unlike him. I knew it could not or would not last. Sure enough, the next day, he countered his own offer by saying: "I've changed my mind! This is my house. You are the one who wants to leave...so you leave. I am staying. And you'll never leave, 'cause you love this house, you designed and decorated it!" he exclaimed in triumph.

When he saw that I was not deterred, he continued: "...and I can't believe that you would dishonor our wedding vows. What's that going to do to your mom and dad, and my mom?" He hit me on every possible vulnerable point that he could. He knew me well enough to know what I held dear. However, instead of weakening my resolve, it only made it stronger.

After two days in the spare room, he suggested that I move back into our bedroom upstairs and he would take over the guest room on the main floor. I knew that I would be trapped upstairs, with no possible escape, and he could guard me from the main floor.

However, he could not stop me from going to work. A week later, my resolve was now stronger, so I phoned my girlfriend Leslie Wellman. Leslie and I had been friends for over ten years, having started out as business associates, and our friendship grew from there, even after she left the Company we were both working for at the time.

After struggling through a divorce and some health issues, Leslie had regained her hold on life, and was living in a condominium in River Heights. Therefore, being the only person that I knew who was divorced, I called her. She was not in, so I left her this bombshell of a message on her answering machine: "Leslie, its Estelle. I need your help. Please call me. It's urgent! I'm leaving John, and I don't know where to go, where to move to...I need your guidance and assistance."

A few hours later, she called back: "Gee whiz, Estelle. That was a heck of a message. What is happening? What is going on? Of course, I'll help," she volunteered, as soon as I filled her in on what had been happening to me throughout the summer. It was now the beginning of September.

John and I were still living in the small town of St. Adolphe, about a half-hour drive from Winnipeg. I had not lived in the city for over 28 years, even though I drove to the office every day, which was situated in the heart of downtown Winnipeg.

I had no idea what was a good neighborhood. Did I need to sign a yearlong lease? A myriad of other questions popped into my mind. I had been scouting out different locations on my own but I was scared of signing a long-term lease.

Leslie immediately reassured me, with an offer that completely took me by surprise: "Why don't you just pack up a suitcase, with enough clothes and stuff for a week or two and move in with me? I have a spare bedroom that you can use until you make up your mind what you really want to do. You can stay a day, a week, a month, or a year! If you decide to go back, no harm done. If you decide to move on, you'll be more prepared."

I took her up on her offer, as a drowning person clings to a piece of driftwood. I went home and told John that I would be leaving soon, I was not sure when. I discussed with him the counseling service that was free of charge, as part of my employee benefits. I suggested that he call the number and make an appointment. He scorned at that and walked out.

My neighbor and friend, Sue Lagasse, offered to help me through the packing and leaving. I felt so numb, the last two days before leaving, that I could barely think. On a Wednesday morning, after John left for work, Sue came over, and we packed up two small suitcases of clothes, took a small four-drawer cardboard storage unit, a few pieces of jewelry, and left the house, not looking back once.

Arriving at Leslie's she held me in her arms and the three of us cried together. Then, Sue and Leslie helped me unpack and settle in her guest room, which would turn out to be my salvation over the next four months.

In the meantime, I was still Regional Manager, attempting to continue working daily and barely holding it together. Some days, I would just sit at my desk, at the office, and tears would start flowing all by themselves. My assistant, Karen Lefebvre, seemed to know by instinct when I was distressed.

She would come by, smile encouragingly, and close my door so that I could break down in private, which I did often in the first month or two. The advice I had given to John to seek out counseling through the Employee Assistance Program, I took as well. I realized that I needed professional help. I knew that I wasn't alone, that every time I felt I couldn't go on, every time I felt the burden of starting over overwhelming; someone would phone, lift my spirits and give me their encouragement.

I had three visits with the Company psychologist, and that helped me tremendously. The first visit, as soon as I walked in, she handed me a box of tissue, and I think I used the whole box in a two-hour session.

The second visit, I only used half a box of tissue. I told her at the end of the session that I must have been making progress, as there was half a box of tissue left over. We both laughed at that. I felt lighter leaving that session.

By the third visit, (these were spread over a two-month period), I hardly cried at all. We focused on going forward, instead of going back. Other women have left relationships in much more dire circumstances than mine. I had a great job, a good salary, with great benefits, my family and friends surrounded me with love and support…I was blessed, indeed.

My sister Monique Piette was one such special person. She and I had always been very close, growing up. Then she married and

moved 1,500 miles away, but that never stopped us from remaining close. I would visit every time my job sent me down East; I would make a point of stopping over for a day or two. We talked on the phone often.

It was with a heavy weight on my shoulders that I called her, the day of my move to Leslie. I announced to her what

I had just done. She was in shock, at first, only because I had never told her how it really was between John and me. She lived far enough away that, when she came to visit, I was able to put on a good front.

Then she said to me, "Now it makes sense! When we stayed at your place two months ago, (when Monique and her husband Hector had come home for their 25th anniversary celebration), I was watching you one morning, when you thought you were alone. I saw the utter despair in the way your shoulders drooped, and the look on your face, until you saw me. Then, your face just lit up, and I thought: My Good, what kind of burden is she carrying?"

She continued: "I want you to come out here for Christmas. You'll need to get away, and it will be too difficult to do all the family get-togethers, with everyone questioning you, so book your tickets now." Therefore, I booked two weeks off work for Christmas in Cornwall, where they lived.

With Monique "in the know," my next move was to tell my parents. How do you tell your 78 year old parents, who themselves have been happily and lovingly married to each other for over 60 years, have raised a family of twelve children, burying one child at age ten, yet had loved and remained devoted to each other to the end?

With a heavy heart, I phoned them to let them know I was coming down for a visit. It is an hour's drive to the senior citizen's complex where they lived, and that was a long, hard drive for me.

When I got there, I sat down on the sofa and taking in a deep breath, said, "Well, Mom and Dad, I have something serious to talk to you about. I've left John, and moved out two days ago."

Mom and Dad looked at each other, stood up and held out their arms to me. We stood there, in the middle of their living room, hugging and kissing each other and crying at the same time.

Dad's lips were trembling, as he told me: "I suspected for the last twelve years, that John wasn't taking care of my little girl."

Mom added, "Are you going to be okay? Do you need any money? What can we do to help you?"

We talked throughout the afternoon, drank gobs of tea, and by the time I left, I felt twenty pounds lighter, knowing that I had not disappointed my parents after all. They loved me and supported me, unconditionally! What a feeling of euphoria, for the first time since I had moved out. "I just might survive this, after all." I thought in complete surprise, as I felt hope rising inside me.

We are a close-knit family, always there for each other. We grew up in a loving, happy home, filled with light, love, and music. Most of the family members can play one to five instruments, have beautiful voices, and some have even been members of country and rock bands over the years.

The ETERNALS

Some of our friends, growing up, included Ron and Ted Palley, of "The Eternals." After school, I can remember Ron coming over and playing "Bumble Boogie" on Mom's piano... he sure could play that instrument, even back then, in 1962. His first band was with his brother Ted Palley, Bobby Everitt, Harry, and Johnny Hildebrand. I so wanted to be in his band, but he told me my voice was not strong enough...it was very diplomatic of him to couch it in those terms.

News of my having moved out got around to my other nine siblings very quickly. Some, I had a chance to phone firsthand. Others had found out through Mom and Dad, but all of them contacted me, to offer support, and love...never the condemnation that I was afraid of hearing from them.

No matter How Far

No matter how far we travel
Towards a hill,
Paying attention to surrounding terrain,
Stone and flower.

We are unprepared
For whatever lies waiting
On the other side.

No one will tell you this:
Our bodies understand
The dreams that are truly our own.

Jack Crimmins

CHAPTER 5

Learning to Cope

Fall 1995

Was it easy? No! After working all day, I would get home to Leslie's condo, collapse on the bed, barely eat, and cry myself to sleep every night. In the morning, sometimes, it was so bad, I felt so drained, that I could barely lift my head off the pillow. I would roll over until I fell off the bed to the floor.

Exhausted, I would stare out the window, at this incredible tree. Looking up into the branches, I watched the sunlight bounding off the bark. Gusts of wind swayed the branches in a rhythmic dance.

I started talking to that tree. I poured out all the pain and agony that I was going through, and started asking the tree to help me, to give me energy to go on.

Then, I started noticing that when I asked, I received. I would start to feel stronger - strong enough to crawl to the shower, let the water pour down on me, sometimes for half an hour, before

 I felt strong enough to get dressed and face the day.

The drab days piled one on top of the other, as I existed in a gray fog, unable to see beyond one day at a time, unable to see a future, or a way to start over. Then, one day, after many weeks had gone by, I woke up one morning, and did not feel like crying! Wow, what a breakthrough day that was!

That weekend, I went to a work-related seminar and met a man, Frank Hunt, from Ottawa. We immediately felt a kinship and started talking. He had been separated for five years and his wife was giving him a hard time about the divorce.

 Frank had been a counselor in the Royal Canadian Air Force, for over 30 years, in the Drug and Alcohol Counseling Unit. He understood where I was coming from and we became friends for "a reason and a season." He was so sympathetic, understanding, and compassionate.

Our nightly telephone conversations were my lifeline. He would listen, and offer his stories as comparisons. He made me see and understand that not all men are the same, and that someday, I would meet someone whom I would trust enough to love again.

Frank had a daughter and granddaughter living in Ottawa. His grand daughter was five years old, and suffering from MS

(Multiple Sclerosis). He was very protective of both of them and would rush her to the hospital at all hours. It was a very stressful time for him as well.

We forged a bond of sorts. I guess because it was over the phone, it was easier to talk to him; it felt more as if I was talking to myself. He mostly listened sympathetically. He did not know any of the parties involved, so it was easier for him to be impartial. Having counseled others daily, he was very in tune to what I was going through, and encouraged me to face it all dead-on.

We met for a purpose, and at that point, I could only hope that our paths would somehow bring us closer together over time. That didn't happen. We had agreed from the start that long-distance relationships most often don't work out. We both moved on with our lives, the richer for having known each other for this brief period.

I had to go see my lawyer to discuss the separation agreement and all it entails. Frankly, I was overwhelmed by what needs to be done over a short period. I went back home and prepared a letter and package for John to look over.

In the meantime, John checked himself in at the psychiatric ward at the Victoria Hospital, and then he called Marc and my girlfriend Sue, who both called me. I cried all night long. I cannot go back - no matter what happens.

I cannot be responsible for his unhappiness or for making him happy. I never could. He never listened, and he still is not listening. When I talked to Frank over the phone the next day, he helped me figure it out that John was doing this as a final effort to get me back.

I felt that if I went to see him at the hospital, it would only delay the inevitable and give him false hope. I talked to Marc, and we decided I would rent a small heated storage space and go to the house while John was in the hospital. I could then get the few things that I wanted, as I had left with only a suitcase of clothes.

At the Caisse Populaire, I took care of financial matters. I re-organized the mortgage payments, paid the yearly taxes, and made it possible for John to continue living in the house for as long as he wanted a home there. I promised myself that I would not call in my half-ownership in the house for as long as he lived there alone. When he got himself a partner, we would decide on the next step.

Marc phoned to say that John would be in the hospital for a few weeks. I felt so sorry for him. I felt his pain. I was in pain also. I was so sad for him, but I knew I could never go back.

We decided that while John was in the hospital, it would be the best time for me to go pick up the rest of my personal belongings and a few pieces of furniture. Saturday morning came and I was so scared to go back into the house. What if I missed home so much that I wanted to go back? Anyway, my two sisters and their husbands: (Colette and Jake, Celine and Jack) and my two best friends (Karen and Sue) were there to help me pack and move my stuff out.

I was so wired; I could feel the "fight or flight" adrenaline. We started sorting through clothes, jewelry, paintings, and in the end, managed to fill Jake's small truck with a few boxes of personal mementos and my personal possessions. I was able to walk out of that house, leaving pretty much everything behind. I never looked back. I breathed a sigh of relief and felt truly free for the first time in twenty-eight years.

The next day, I woke up bone weary. I was aching all over from the stress and tension of yesterday's move, until Frank called and made me laugh. I could just picture his blue eyes sparkling when he is telling a funny story. He is one neat person.

I kept asking him what is in it for him, while I am going through all this. He says he is enjoying it too...the teasing without being ridiculed, the exchanging of ideas. We talked about things besides my impending divorce and it was so nice to share discussions without always being on guard. He taught me to move on, slowly but progressively.

Frank had a wicked sense of humor. I would love to hear him laugh. He loved golf, but refused to take himself seriously. He was smart and sensitive - a loving, caring individual and a Pisces, like me.

He talked about his daughter Sherry, and his two darling granddaughters Kelsey and Melissa. When he talked about his baby granddaughter Kelsey, I could feel his pain over her very serious illness. She might not live to be 10 years old, he mentioned to me, with sadness and resignation in his voice.

My girlfriend and housemate, Leslie Wellman, had to go to the hospital for minor surgery. I took her there and back and settled her down in bed with a "bed picnic." I spread a picnic tablecloth on the bed, and then put out an array of munchies....grapes, cheese and crackers, smoked salmon, some cheezies, chocolates.

My bird Sammy was downstairs chirping away as he hated being left alone in a room. Therefore, I went to get him and brought him up on my shoulder. He had a picnic with us. We were both feeding him pieces of grapes, and he loved the cheezies, so we were giving him small pieces of that as well.

All of a sudden, he sneezed and upchucked (if a bird can do that); shaking his head and sending stuff flying all over me, Leslie, the walls behind her. We laughed so hard we thought her stitches were going to open up.

I took Marc and Lizanne out for their fourth Anniversary dinner, and had a wonderful time. I felt so lucky to have them in my life. I loved both of them so much. We talked about all the things we were thankful for and all they have accomplished in four short years. It was amazing.

My friend Ian Dark invited me to join his office staff at a Blue Bomber dinner. Ian had recently been widowed, when his wife had a sudden and fatal heart attack while talking to him on the phone. It had been a shocking time for him, and so he could relate to what I was going through. He asked how I was doing, and I told him it is tougher than anything you can imagine did, but I would do it all over again to get to this point in my life.

One night, my girlfriend Karen Lefebvre and her three boys came over to watch movies with me. She was (and is) a great friend. We had so much in common and explored different ideas together. It was very stimulating being around her. We watched a movie about finding love and destiny. We discussed that although we both did not have great first marriages, that it didn't mean we were prepared to go it alone for the rest of our lives.

My brother Ron came over to visit quite often. He had gone through a painful divorce himself and so he could relate to what I was going through. He offered encouragement and support each and every visit.

It made me reflect on where I go from here. Was I prepared to go it alone for the rest of my life or was I prepared to spend my life searching for some-one who is meant to be with me.

Every morning, when I woke up, I sat on the floor, looking at this strong tree outside. I would visualize my circle of friends and family around me, keeping me strong. I saw: Grandfather, Marc and Lizanne, Monique & Hector, Celine and Jack, Colette and Jake, Vic and May, Ron, Karen, Sue, Frank, Bill, Monica, Fabe, Caterina, Diane, Steve, and Kathy.

I asked for their positive energy and love, to help keep me strong and to help me make it through the days and nights ahead. I had been having asthma attacks, and going back to the doctor again. He checked and my lungs were OK. He gave me a prescription for relaxants to help me sleep and for my cough. He hugged me. Dr. McGowan and I had been through a lot together… he had been my doctor since I was 18 years old. He delivered Marc. He had always been there for me, never letting me down.

As the months went by, I could see that I was making progress. I was getting stronger, mentally and physically. While attending a meeting at our Head Office in Burlington, my boss offered me a job transfer to another province. I had not even considered such a move, but instead of saying no, I heard myself say, "Let me phone my son, and I'll talk to you later on in the day."

Therefore, I called my son Marc: "Honey, I've just been offered a job transfer to another Province…Calgary, Alberta. What do you think? Should I take it?"

I asked him.

"Well, Mom," Marc replied, "this might be the best thing for you at this time. It will be a fresh start. You'll make new friends. We would go visit you often. We both love downhill skiing, and you're moving in that area."

"You don't think that I'm deserting you, then, if I take this transfer?" I asked anxiously. I knew that our divorce had been tough on him and that John had not been easy on him either.

When I moved out, I had not left any phone number or address where I would be living. Marc and my family knew where to reach me, but I had asked that no one provide John with that information. John knew that Marc knew where I was living, and he had harassed him constantly to get my address and phone number.

John told Marc: "Well, now that I know that your Mom's serious about leaving me, I want to get her back. I guess the political thing I should have done was to say yes to do the vacuuming. I want her back, now!"

My wise son told his dad: "Dad, you know when you've lost a hockey game, and you look at the rerun, you say at one point: 'Gee, I could have scored there, but I did not. I had another opportunity to score again...but I did not. No matter how many times you replay the game, at the end...you still lost that game.' Dad...this game is over! Maybe the next one, you can do it differently, but this one is over. Mom's not coming back."

When John realized that this was serious, this was IT...he fell apart. He checked himself into the hospital, and stayed in the psychiatric ward for over a month. He would phone me at work, to add to my own burdens, to tell me that I was responsible for this as well.

However, during my counseling sessions, my counselor made me come to the realization that I was only human and not responsible for anyone's happiness or unhappiness, but my own! What a liberating session that was.

I got a call from the psychiatric nurse, asking me to go to joint counseling with John, that it was the only way to help him. I replied, "No, I can't do that. I can barely manage my own pain and grief. I cannot be of any help to John at this time."

Marc called me about an hour later, to say he had received the same call, and he had answered the same thing that I did. This was something that John had to learn to do for himself. No one could do it for him.

The decision was made. I was moving to Calgary, Alberta in December 1995.

I could not quite believe that I had made such a life-changing decision. On my own, far from my family and friends (except for my brother Vic and his wife May who lived in Calgary, thank God). What was I doing?

John had bought me a bird two years earlier...a cockatiel named Sam. Because we did not know its gender for the first six months, I chose the name Sam...for either Samuel or Samantha, depending on what it turned out to be. It turned out to be a Samuel.

 Although it was my bird, he responded extremely well to John. He ate his toast with him every morning, and would fly to his shoulder as soon as John walked into the room. When I left John, it was difficult to leave Sammy behind, but I thought that he would be a good companion to John and that it was the right thing to do, so I reluctantly said goodbye to my little feathered friend.

Sammy was a special little bird. He was hand-raised and we got him when he was two months old. He did not know how to fly yet and his wings had been clipped. One Saturday, I had taken him outside in the back yard, as it was a calm, clear day. I took him out of his cage and put him on my rock garden. He walked around chirping and pecking. It was so cute. He made me laugh. John came out to see what I was laughing about and he laughed too.

The next day, it was very windy, and I was sitting outside on the patio, when John comes walking out with Sammy on his head. I screamed at John, "Don't come out with him, it's too windy!" However, it was too late. Sammy had spread his wings and taken off in the wind. He was gone!

We were both starring at the sky, where Sammy had disappeared, and sat down in shock. "Omigod, he'll never find his way back here." I started wailing. "He doesn't even know how to fly or how to land." John felt bad about it. I put Sammy's cage in the back yard; on the off chance that Sammy might fly back, recognize his back yard and cage.

How do you go searching for a bird? My girlfriend Sue and I would go walking every night, looking at every tree in town, and whistling for Sammy. Well, it turned cold that week, and snowed for a few nights. I despaired, took the birdcage into the house, and put it away in the storage room.

I suggested we put up a sign at the post office and general store, just in case. John negated that suggestion, so Sammy was not mentioned again. Ten days went by, and I got a phone call from John at work, "Do you believe in miracles?" he asks me excitedly. "Of course I do." I replied.

"Well," he explained, "I just got a call from the people who live two blocks away from us, and they captured a tame bird in their back yard. They think it might be Sammy!"

This woman just happened to look out her window and saw this little bird on one of her bushes. He looked wounded and she did not know what to do. Her neighbor, however, was an environmentalist, so she came over immediately. She knew what to do. She carried a box, with a stick pushed through both sides, had some birdseeds and water in the box, and when she approached Sammy, he just fell into her hands, in total exhaustion.

She put him in the box, closed the lid, and took him home. Then she started phoning around to see who had lost a bird recently. Someone finally mentioned our name, so she had phoned John to confirm that it was indeed our bird.

We went to pick him up and took him home; took him out of the box and put him back in his familiar cage and covered him up with a big, heavy blanket. He was in shock, and we did not know if he would live or not, so we just let him recover quietly. His feathers had been pecked at around his neck, while being attacked by other birds, and his mouth was bloody as well. Moreover, he was only four months old!

Two days went by, and then I heard a little "chirp," then a stronger "chirp" and when I pulled off the blanket, there he was at the door of his cage! After that episode, you can understand my reluctance to leave my little bird behind…but I did.

Then, to my surprise, a few weeks later, Marc phoned to say that John did not want the responsibility of taking care of Sammy and that if I did not come to pick him up immediately, that he would give him away. Well, Leslie and I jumped into my car, drove over to the house, and picked up Sammy.

Now Sammy was living with Leslie and me. Sammy was used to having his cage door open and he could come and go as he pleased in the house. However, Leslie was not used to that. He would fly at her and attack her fingers. It was hilarious! (Well, to me, anyway, if not to Leslie). She would then threaten Sammy, as she was frying chicken, that he would be the next meal in the frying pan. I kept telling her that Sammy understood what she was saying, which was why he was constantly attacking her!

As the fall progressed, the leaves turned colors and started to fall. I felt the change happening in me as well. As the winter snows came, and Christmas approached, I prepared to go to Cornwall for Christmas, followed by a move to Calgary in early January.

I reflected on the many steps that I hade taken since leaving John. I was moving to Calgary end-December, I was buying a condominium in Calgary, and I was letting go of the daily calls to Frank in Ottawa. It was time to move on for both of us. We reflected on the difficult times we had gone through. It had been a time of courage and growth.

I told him I felt good about the direction my life was taking after so much turmoil, fear, and paralysis. Things were now happening at a very quick pace, and that's OK. I was ready for it and I felt I could handle it. I wanted to experience life to the fullest, live, and love. I had no regrets. It was simply time to move on to the next phase of my life and time for John to move on in his own direction as well.

I was afraid…sometimes feeling paralyzed by the fear. I came across a copy of the book: "Feel the Fear…and Do It Anyways." I read it while in Cornwall, started meditating and asking for help from all my friends, my little brother Richard and my grandfather Willie, both of whom were on the other side.

December 1995

The two weeks in Cornwall were incredibly healing for me. To be with my sister, Monique, who was later to be identified by a medium as "golden...a golden child of God." Monique and Hector were unbelievably kind, understanding, and supportive.

One night, Hector and I started drinking wine, and I was pouring my heart out, which was getting more pathetic with each glass of wine. Monique finally gave up on us, in disgust, and went to bed. Well, Hector and I carried on drinking more wine, and at one point, the conversation went like this: "...and you know, Hector, that I left everything behind at the house. When I went back to get a few things (books, pictures, one small love seat, a wicker chair, one television set, the rest of my clothes)...I asked John to go through everything, and whatever he didn't want, my girlfriend Sue would pack it up for me.

"Well, he didn't give me one thing more. He sold it all at a garage sale, rather than let me have anything else (pots, pans, whatever)..." I rambled on. "...And you know what the worst thing is, Hector?" I asked, in my inebriated state. "He never even let me have one tool...not one of his five hammers, not one of his three drills, no tools"! I ended on a desolate note.

Anyone who knows our family would appreciate the humor in

that statement. We come from a carpenter family…my grand-father was a carpenter, my dad was a carpenter, some of my brothers are carpenters, and Hector is a carpenter himself, working for the Cornwall School Division.

Hector was shocked at the news…no tools! Well, we were almost crying at that point (two o'clock in the morning and a few bottles of wine later). The next day, we were nursing a slight hangover. We were getting absolutely no sympathy from Monique (and rightly so!).

The rest of the stay proceeded with a shopping trip to the States and Boxing Day bargains where I bought my first 8-piece set of stainless steel cutlery. I carried that set with me on the plane back to Manitoba…my very first purchase for the new condominium that I had bought in Calgary in November.

Yes, I had actually bought a condo in Calgary. The company that I worked for sent me on a house-hunting mission in November. I called my brother Vic, and his wife May, who were both retired and who kindly volunteered to help me find a place. At first, I thought I should rent an apartment but, after looking for two days, my brother finally got me to admit that I was not too keen on that idea. We switched gears and got a hold of a real estate agent. I contacted our Head Office relocating department, and found out how much I could afford. I was most fortunate that my company, CUMIS Insurance, financed my mortgage, and handled all the real estate costs.

Based on that information, the real estate agent got very focused and we went through thirty condominiums in three days. I loved the first one that we saw but she would not let me think about it until I had seen many more. At the end of the three days, you guessed it, we went back to see the first one and a new one across the street had just come on the market.

May spotted it and pointed it out to the agent. We went to see it and fell in love with it. It was facing south, had a bay window in the living room and in the kitchen, which looked out over a park-like area. There were three bedrooms on the upper level and a fully professionally designed lower level – decorated in all my favorite colors (green, taupe, and wine). After some quick back and forth negotiations, I signed the mortgage documents for my very own first condominium. It was an incredible rush!

After Christmas in Cornwall, I flew back to Winnipeg to prepare for an early January move to Calgary; and to a fresh, new start!

PART II

Moving On

THE BLEAKNESS OF WINTER NIGHT

I can just about get through the day
However, the night makes me nervous.
Not for any reason
Except maybe that, it catches you unaware
And follows you the way a man follows
When he wants something.

I've been in every kind of night
So I shouldn't be afraid of darkness
But still the night makes me nervous.

Rod McKuen

CHAPTER 6

The Big Move

January 1996

I had asked Leslie to drive to Calgary with me, and I would fly her back to Winnipeg. So on a bleak; extremely cold, blustery day in January, we started out on our trek to Calgary, with Sammy's cage tied up in the back seat of the car.

We had planned to stay overnight in Regina, Saskatchewan, due to the short and very cold winter days and we arrived there in the waning light of day. Arriving at Hotel Saskatchewan, upon registering I inquired about Sammy, as to where could he be housed overnight. The staff was marvelous. They brought a round table and beautifully draped linen to the floor, set Sammy's cage in the middle, and there he was…little king of the hotel suite.

The next day, we crossed the border between Saskatchewan and Alberta.

On the road, Sammy suddenly started chirping away. I opened his cage door. He flew out and landed on the steering wheel,

where he started looking left, right, and fluffing out his feathers, as if he was driving the car. Well, Leslie and I just lost it…we laughed so hard; we had tears in our eyes.

Sammy drove the car for a few hours, until he got tired, fluttered back to his cage, and promptly fell asleep. We arrived at my brother's house in the late afternoon, and settled in for the night. In a few days, the moving van would be arriving with the few possessions that I had brought with me from Winnipeg.

The first order of Day One, I explained to Vic and his wife May, after dropping Leslie off at the air-port, as she had to get back to her job in Winnipeg, was to get myself a bedroom suite and then a kitchen suite. May, being the queen bee of shopping in Calgary, started hunting for sales, and away we went. By the end of the day, I had bought a bedroom suite and a kitchen suite, both of which would be delivered the next day.

Day Two, the first look at my condominium felt wonderful. Then the delivery vans started arriving, and it was non-stop all day, getting the furniture moved in, unpacked, more shopping for pillows, linens, and all the stuff to make a bed.

In the kitchen were a table and four chairs and not much else – except oh yeah, my stainless steel cutlery set that I had bought in Cornwall at Christmas.

Day 3, the moving van arrived from Winnipeg and unloaded the love seat, television and stereo system, a wicker chair and wicker coffee table, a few pictures, my clothes and that was pretty much it. The living room and dining room were completely empty, and our voices echoed throughout the emptiness. Nevertheless, I was in my own home at last and it felt wonderful!

My brother-in-law Hector had given me a box before I left Cornwall at Christmas, wrapped up with a note that said, "Open when you get to your condo in Calgary." I had left it with the movers, so when I got to that box, I quickly opened it, and there was a Makita cordless drill inside. Well, I hugged it to my heart, and started crying. It was such a beautiful gesture on Hector's part, to ensure that I would have my own tools. How thoughtful!

"You're going to sleep over at our place for a few more nights, 'because I know you're going to be scared in new surroundings, alone for the first time in your life," Vic stated emphatically.

"No," I replied. "I'm going to start out in my own place, my own new bed, and bring lots of comfort food and magazines with me to bed, so if I can't sleep, I'll read away the night fears. Eventually, I'll be so tired, I'm bound to sleep." I continued, with more bravado than I actually felt. "Besides," I added, laughingly, "I've got Sammy to protect me."

Vic and May reluctantly left me there alone that first night and I was almost disappointed the next morning when I woke up to sunshine through the bedroom window, and Sammy chirping beside the bed. I had slept the entire night through, without even waking up once.

The pattern was set. Because it was winter, cold and dark early, I did not get to see any neighbors for the first few months. I started working at the Calgary office, and was putting in fourteen-hour days, trying to reorganize the office space, the staff, the regional office in Edmonton, and the one in Calgary. It was a huge task and completely absorbed most of my time and energy. On my way home from work, I would stop at Home Depot and pick up something from the long list of things to do at the condominium. I occupied myself sewing curtains, putting up shelves, organizing a home office, and so on - starting a new life for myself.

Vic & May lent me two chairs and a side table for the living room, which I appreciated using until I got the chance to get what I really wanted.

It was a lonely, bleak time. I will not kid you. I was still struggling with depression. Some mornings, I had to throw myself off the bed onto the floor and crawl to the door; I could barely get up. Instead of fighting this early morning phenomenon, I decided to work with it.

I would crawl to the end of the bed, where I had a white candle, which I would light. Then, I would ask God for help. I would ask that he send someone into my life to lift me up. I would then ask the spirits of my beloved grandfather "Willie," my angel brother Richard, and all of my other related spirits to form a circle of protection around me. Then, I would visualize all of my living, powerful positive friends around me. I would name them and form a circle around the other spirits. I would ask my living friends to send me their energy and support as well. By the time I was finished, I would start to feel strong enough to stand up and face the day.

After working all day, as soon as I drove into my parking stall in front of the condominium, I would hear Sammy starting to chirp, welcoming me home. I would open his cage door and he would hop out onto my shoulder, come down to my chin, and bury his little head underneath my chin. He allowed me to snuggle him with my chin only. I knew never to touch a bird on their feathers as it leaves an oily residue that can be harmful to them.

Sammy and I would sit on the floor in the living room, in front of the wood fireplace. While burning a few logs that the previous tenants had so graciously left me, I'd tell Sammy: "Well, Sammy, if this is the worst that it gets…alone, it's dark and cold outside, with no furniture, it's not too bad, eh?" I would watch Sammy strut across the expanse of the living room floor and smile. For the first time in a long time, I was at peace.

Being single helped me learn who I was. After six months of "singleness," I saw that this time had allowed me to turn my attention towards my passions, my friends, and my career. It had been about learning who I am, not through a man, but for myself.

That being said, it takes time to come to terms with your new "single" status. This process is not something you want to rush. I focused on my new "singleness" positively – allowed myself to spend time alone and not rush to fill the emptiness with "busyness," not fight the loneliness, but embrace it fully.

During that bleak first winter in Calgary, I reflected a lot on my life…who was I exactly? I had pretended for so long, I had forgotten my likes and dislikes. I got to know me all over again. "I am not ordinary. I'm unique - all people are unique. So, why are we here?" I would ask during some of these navel gazing sessions with myself. I had always been a reader, so filled my nights alone reading books...Betty Eadie, Deepak Chopra, Marianne Williamson, and other authors of new age and spiritual thinking.

I thought back to reflections from childhood, ripping my tongue on barbed wire fence (I can still taste the metal in my mouth when I think of it); dad throwing himself on the floor when he would come in from work, claiming he was too tired to undress himself. We would all pile up on top of him, pulling at his boots, his cap, and his coat. Then, we would hear the crinkling sound of a candy bag coming from somewhere, and there would be a frenzy to see who would find the candy first. He would roll over and laugh until we found it, and then made sure that everyone had a piece of candy. Sweet moments indeed!

Mom and dad were phoning me once a week, concern in their voice, and always asking me if I was in need of anything, and did I need any money? They could not understand that I had left everything behind, that my husband was living in our house back in Manitoba, that I was starting out from nothing, and that I was in no need of anything. I reassured them that I was earning a good salary and had enough to look after my basic needs and wants.

The telephone was my only link to my personal world. Most nights, I would phone Monique, or vice-versa. She was always encouraging, supportive, and providing insights as we discussed books, religion, and other subjects.

It was very helpful to me, during this season, while my heart was healing.

Before I knew it, four months had passed by, the days were getting longer, the weather was warming up, and spring had arrived. I had done quite a bit of work on the condominium. The kitchen was all set. Sammy was happy; he had a great view of the outdoors from his "Tajmahal" birdcage.

I started to meet some of my neighbors. One couple, Dee and Moe, became very good friends.

One day, while we were having coffee, Dee mentioned that her neighbor across the street was also a single woman, from Winnipeg, and that she would arrange for us to meet.

That is how I met Suzanne Zonneveld. We took to each other right away, and she has become one of my very best and dearest friends to this day. Suzanne had moved from Winnipeg a year earlier to complete her Masters in Family Counseling at the University of Calgary.

Whenever I had a hard day at the office, or her thesis was not coming together the way she wanted; we would call each other, pop open a bottle of wine and talk.

Suzanne would suggest books to read and then we would discuss them and share our hopes, dreams, disappointments, and so on. She is fun and smart.

Suzanne had one married daughter living in Calgary, and one married son back in Winnipeg. She was widowed at age 28, when her beloved husband Peter had cancer. She raised her two children alone, never remarried, and now, in her early fifties, was pursuing her dream of completing her Master's Degree in Nursing – Family Counseling.

It was inspiring to hear of her overcoming her trials and tribulations, and somehow made my situation seem lighter. As I listened, I opened my heart to allow in change.

Another friend, Melody Jones, from Regina, called one day and I asked her to come out for a few days visit, which she did.

Melody was the Human Resources Manager for the West and we both worked for the same company. We had developed a friendship outside of work as well. We explored Banff and Calgary antique shops. That was a fun!

Melody had been studying alternative healing methods for years and made annual treks to California, studying under Dr. Theresa Dale, and bringing back awesome healing programs. While she was visiting, I took one of her courses, and from that moment on, was on the search for more and more.

I took the Reality Management Program, with Melody. This program is designed to put you back in control of your life. This course provided me with the tools I needed to explore and eliminate the cause of any life condition that was not serving my highest good. I learned that we all have the ability to create the reality that we desire. Through this program, I was able to align myself with my goals and create my dreams of self-empowerment.

It focused on taking an issue, finding out what element is out of balance, test which emotion is tied to the issue, feel it and release it, and then replace it with a positive new thought and emotion regarding the same issue. What a great course and awesome techniques to use to move out of negative zones and focus on the positive. This knowledge was truly life changing for me. To learn more about Melody's amazing programs, visit her website:

After she left and I had worked with her program for a few weeks, I wrote her this letter:

"Dear Melody,

Although I had done some work with you privately, prior to taking the Reality Management Program, I still was not prepared for the impact that this program would make in my life. The power of this program is so awesome that it became downright scary to use it after the course ended. However, in further discussions with you and following your advice to work on the "fear of using the program" this issue was resolved.

You have been a wonderful influence in my life over the past two years especially. Thank you so much for your guidance, support, and assistance during this very difficult but enriching and liberating year that I've just travelled. I know there will be more challenging times ahead for both of us, as we enter different phases of our lives. However, with the Reality management Program tools at our disposal, I know and visualize success and happiness for both of us in our new ventures.

Many thanks, Estelle"

YOU CAME

You came like spring
and lit my soul on fire
when the birds began to sing
you came and inspired
When the flowers began to bloom
with the smell of spring in the air
you took away the gloom
and taught me how to care

I'll never be the same
you breathed new life into me
I'm so glad you came
A true friend you'll always be

Lynn Smiley

CHAPTER 7

Spring Brings New Hope

D ee and Moe introduced me to another of their friends, Cameron Wood, who had been a psychiatric nurse for over 17 years. He was currently in private care, looking after one patient, a boy in his late teens, who was severely handicapped, having been born of an alcohol mother. The way that Cameron handled his duties with his patient was amazing. Cameron had taught him sign language, as he could not speak. He treated his patient with kindness, humor, and incredible patience, the likes of which I had never seen before.

Cameron loves birds. He sees beauty in nature, not just the natural beauty that everyone sees, but the small "insignificant to others" type of beauty… like a bird's nest, like a spider's web. He is a photographer. His nature photography has won him numerous awards. He is a sensitive soul, who has been hurt badly, but is not bitter.

He told me that he had applied to move to Korea to teach English as a Second Language and that he would be leaving Calgary, probably for good, in about nine months. I was sad to hear that, as we had become good friends, but I understood his desire. Cam was also an avid reader. Most of his life, he had been fascinated by eastern culture and religion. This was his lifetime opportunity to explore this part of the world.

Cam taught me a lot during the time that we spent together. On Sunday afternoons, we would drive to a nearby park, bring some birdseed along, and hold our hand out filled with birdseed, patiently waiting until the chickadees trusted us enough to come and eat out of our hands, which they did. It was so peaceful and rewarding for me, to sit in absolute silence for hours, feeding the birds, enjoying each other's company.

During one of my conversations with Suzanne, about there being no such thing as "coincidence", I mentioned to her wasn't it amazing that, from the moment I left John, that three people in the medical field had come into my life. Apart from herself, there was Frank Hunt, from Ottawa; and Cameron Wood, from Calgary.

Prior to that, I had never encountered anyone in the medical field…how strange. How amazing! The Power of Three.

Spring had arrived and I had made a few new friends, I had good colleagues at work and the condominium was "a work in progress." I had managed to get the bedroom completed.

Then I met Stan and Karen Lopston, the couple living across the street from my condominium, also from Winnipeg. Suddenly, I no longer felt alone. Other 'Peggers surrounded me.

Marc and Lizanne came out for their first visit, in spring of 1996. I took them skiing at Lake Louise, along my brother Vic and his daughter Chantelle, who are all avid downhill skiers.

While they were doing the black and blue runs, I signed up for a group lesson on downhill skiing…that was a dismal failure! I failed to graduate to the towrope…something the 6-year olds were doing after a half-hour lesson. Methinks a downhill skier I will not be. At least, I would not have to worry about attempting skiing until the next winter.

Marc & Lizanne were grinning and whispering to each other then announced "Mom...we have great news to share with you...we're expecting our first child in September." I jumped up and hugged them both: "What joyous news! I am so thrilled for all of us. Imagine that...I will be a grandmother before I am fifty years old. I'm so ready!" I enthused.

Driving them to the airport was always very difficult, not knowing when I would see them again. Nevertheless, I but on a brave face, a "stiff upper lip" until the plane was in the sky. Only then would I allow the tears to come. It was hard to drive back to the empty condominium that had been so full of life, laughter, and love during their visit.

It was hard not to get depressed after their visit. I was so fortunate to have Suzanne nearby, who would come over and cheer me up. We would focus on the positives...like the thought of being a grandparent, going back to Winnipeg after the birth, and preparing a baby shower.

I introduced Karen and Suzanne to the joys of "garage sales." I convinced them to come with me, every Saturday morning. We would scour the neighborhood, for treasures and furniture to fill up my condominium. They would arrive on my doorstep, at nine a.m. sharp, with their travel mugs of coffee and away we would go. If anyone asked...we were "gone sale-ing."

My brother Vic and his wife May and I had gone to Bragg Creek to do some sightseeing, and in one of the shops was this gorgeous wrought iron metalwork wine rack, which was about five feet high by two feet wide. The price tag was around $600. I wanted to buy it. Vic talked me out of it, so I did not…but I could not stop thinking and talking about it for weeks after.

Well, one Saturday sale-ing day, Karen spots a wine rack very similar to the one I had described to her. We strategized. I got her to stand guard, because the place was packed, while I went to hunt down the owner. I asked her the price, and she quoted $125. I was ecstatic inside, but putting on an "indifferent" face, asked if she would accept $75. She said yes. We backed up the car and loaded that piece up in a jiffy - that was one of my best garage sale buys. Vic could not believe it when he saw the iron wine rack, with doors, for that price.

 The only other garage sale buy to top that was a few years earlier, in Winnipeg, my sister Celine and I were doing garage sale-ing, and happened onto an estate sale that was so huge, it was mind boggling. We were both exhausted, and it was nearing the end of the morning, on our way home. There were about five tables of jewelry, and scanning quickly through it, I picked up a silver bracelet, about two inches wide, that was made up of both polished and beaten silver on it. I asked the price, and offered $6.00, which was accepted. I brought the bracelet home, thinking if it lasted a few months before it fell apart, that would be fine with me. However, it never did.

A year later, I was visiting a girlfriend in Toronto, wearing that bracelet. We went to an antique jewelry sale, and at one counter, this woman grabbed me by the arm and asked, "Oh, my God…is that bracelet the real thing? Can I take a look at the inside inscription?" she continued excitedly: "We wondered if that bracelet was ever going to show up. Look at this book…here is that bracelet…and yours is the real thing. However did you get this?" She almost fainted when I said a garage sale in Winnipeg for $6.00. She suggested that I get it appraised and insured immediately, which I did after returning to Winnipeg. It was appraised at $750. (And that was in 1990).

I now had bragging rights to being called the "guru of garage sales"…and proud of it. In garage sales, as in life, I came to appreciate and enjoy the highs, and accept the lows.

During that time, I had reduced my body weight by twenty pounds. In one of our discussions about body weight, Suzanne and I concluded that women have a hard time losing weight… because we are not "losers." We have been trained to be organized, multi-taskers, super moms, super wives; therefore, we are not losers…small wonder we cannot lose weight.

So, when you are thinking about weight, think in terms of "reducing your body weight," instead of "losing weight," which has such a negative connotation.

A SUMMER DAY

In the wide valleys, lone and fair,
Lyrics are piped from limpid air,
And, far above, the pine trees free
Voice ancient lore of sky and sea.
Come; let us fill our hearts straightway
With hope and courage of the day.

Noon, hiving sweets of sun and flower,
Has fallen on dreams in wayside bower,
Where bees hold honeyed fellowship
With the ripe blossom of her lip;
Where idleness is gathered up
A magic draught in summer's cup.

Lucy Maud Montgomery

CHAPTER 8

A Wealth of Visitors

1996

With summer came a wealth of visitors from back home, and a host of friends from across the country came to visit me and the beautiful Rocky Mountains, which are only one hour's drive away from Calgary. I had now completed decorating the television room.

Melody came to visit in May for a few days. Suzanne, Melody, and I went to Lake Louise on a daylong hike up to the teahouse. We would stop and meditate along the way. It was a wonderful day.

We were talking about guardian angels and angel guides when Melody told me she knew her angel guides by name and that she had found out through automatic writing[3]. I asked her if she could

---

[3] Automatic Writing has been accepted as a way of communication with the spirits, through the utilization of an implement - a computer or pen and paper. In automatic writing, you record as well as ask pertinent questions, once you establish contact. For more information on Automatic Writing, using any search engine, type in "Automatic Writing."

find out any information of my guides for me, and she said she would try, so we left it at that.

The next morning, I walked into the kitchen, and there was an entire page hand-written on the kitchen table, with the following:

Introduction to Estelle's spirit guides

Guardian Angel – Fieronan (fee-on-an)

This is a wonderful soul whose name signifies the ferocity with which he chooses to take his guarding of you. It is truly his joy to allow you the growth and room that you need to learn your lessons and grow spiritually, while still protecting you from all hard. You need to begin to call on your guardian angel more and more as the coming times begin to unravel. There will be many changes as you begin to get in touch with your life lessons and chosen paths and with this in mind, you must begin to call on Fieronan for guidance and assistance. All you need to do is ask for his help and he will be there to provide answers, support, love, and protection.

Angel of Hope – Pherystalion (per-sta-lon)

This angel is very timid and appears only in the hours of desperation and total darkness of the soul. She has been around much lately, because of all that you have needed to identify with and feel hope for in your life. Pherystalion is a wonderful soul who loves and cares deeply and it is through this commitment to the human spirit that she has come to bond with you. Your tremendous passion and commitment to humanity is well noted and that is why you were given such a special angel of hope.

Angel of Friendship – Frouglishyn (froo-gah-li-shn)

This angel is fierce and loyal and replicates that which you feel for your special friends. You have many friends, but only a few special friends and it is with this angel's help that you have created such a loving bond towards those people. You sometimes allow people into your life that should not be there. With this in mind, the next while will be spent trying to release that which creates attraction from those who would choose to detract from your friendships, rather than add to them. This angel will assist you in making conscious new choices regarding friendship, and with his help, those who do not serve you will fall away as friends.

Angel of Love – Justina

This angel is very loving, kind, and brilliant in color. Whenever you feel love, which you feel very intensely because of your tremendous capacity for love, your heart is filled with the love and light of God as directed by Justina. It is through Justina that your heart is so open, loving, and kind, and with her help will strengthen that area. You need to pay special attention to your soul mates; they will begin to play a much larger picture in your life and are there for very special reasons. The bond that one creates has, and feels with their soul mates is like no other and is not to be taken lightly. With this in mind, for we know that you take nothing about love lightly, you must begin to focus more on these people and allow the position that they are to take in your life and the lesson that they are to provide you with and the connection that naturally exists there, to be strengthened at all times and in all area.

Angel of Happiness – Rose

This very special heavenly body has been manifested out of the growing happiness in your heart. You have broken the mold of old programming that allowed you to be kept down and it is with your new growth in mind that a new heavenly messenger was dispatched to teach you how to be happy. Your heart is truly happy now, although you have periods of remorse or confusion, in your soul there is true joy and we see and feel that, and are truly happy for you and how you have grown over the past while to be exactly where you are now.

Angel of Finances – Bustonian

This angel will play a very special role in your life within the next little while. There is much for you to do and there will be the money you require to do it. Your home is your sanctuary and with this in mind, it is only fitting that it be equipped exactly as you choose. This angel will assist you with your choices, purchases, and decisions regarding buying."

I just sat there reading and re-reading this information, in total awe of what Melody had done during the night. When she came downstairs a few hours later, I hugged her and thanked her. "For what?" she asks, in the middle of a yawn. "For this," I waved the pages she had written during the night. She looks at the pages: "Oh, that is my writing, but I don't remember anything about it. When I ask for assistance, I never remember doing it."

I have never felt alone from that moment on, because I know my spirit guides surround me with their love and protection, guidance and support. How more blessed can I be?

Suzanne, Karen, and I were still doing our "garage saleing" every Saturday morning. One such garage sale day, both Karen and I were bidding for the same brass animal, so we came up with a challenge that whoever got the most small brass animals by the end of the summer, would have to cook the other a seven-course meal. Of course, I threatened that mine would be a six-pack of beer and a hot dog! The bet was on.

Every week, we would display our purchases on the ledge of our bay windows. Our neighbors heard of the bet and walked by our places, keeping score. This went on for the entire spring and summer; the deadline was September 30.

My girlfriend Kathy Hammond came out from Hamilton, Ontario in June for a visit. Many other friends and family from across the country came that summer to visit me and the mountains that were only one hour's drive away.

I felt like I was starting to live again, and enjoy life. It was a full summer with many day trips and a full slate of visitors. Hotel Estelle was in full swing!

Then, one day, I received a letter from my ex-husband John. Just seeing his familiar handwriting on the envelope filled me with foreboding. I was actually scared to open it. I could feel the negative vibes emanating from the package. It was a ten-page letter.

I sat at the kitchen table, took a deep breath, and started to read. I read two paragraphs and I started to cry uncontrollably. It was so full of venom and hatred towards me...why? I had never done or said anything to hurt him. I just wanted to be free to live my own life. Why couldn't he accept that? He was very bitter and accused me of having left him for another man. Then, when he found out that, no, I wasn't with anyone, he was even more incensed and insulted that I would dare leave him for myself.

And that was in the first half of the first page. Then, my brother Vic just happened to phone. When he heard my voice, he immediately asked, "What's wrong?" I told him.

"Put it down," he said, "and wait until I get there. I'll be there in 30 minutes." I put the letter down and made fresh coffee.

When Vic arrived, he sat down. "Okay...now read the letter." I read the letter. Then he read the letter. He shook his head, took my two hands in his, and said, "Estelle...never mind the letter. He is trying to hurt you every way and any way that he can. He wants a reaction from you. But...what do you want?"

I looked at him and said, "To be free, to be me."

"Well, then, fold that letter up, burn it in the fireplace, ignore that you ever received it and focus on your goal. You wanted to be free, and you are. You don't need to reply to him. Just let it go. All the hurtful things he said about you, about mom and dad, about the family...it's all meant to get a reaction from you. He knows your weaknesses, and he aimed right for them. So, just ignore it, and let it go. That's the hardest thing you have to do. Can you do that?"

I nodded. "Yes, you're so right. I'm so glad you came over. You have shown me that I am free of him, and this simply just proves it. Thank you for being there for me."

"You know, Vic," I continued, "you've been there for me when it really counted in my life. Remember when you saved me from drowning when I was only five years old? We had gone on a family picnic at our Uncle Delphise's farm. There was a river, with a bridge across where the picnic was taking place. In my five year old wisdom, I decided to walk across the water back to the picnic instead of going across on the bridge."

Well, the current swept me away, and my brother Vic, who was five years older than I was, saw my long hair floating by, and jumped in, grabbed my hair and pulled me out. That was the first gateway for me.

Apparently, everyone has five gateways back to the other side. These are times in your life when you have a choice to make…you can go back home to the other side, or you can stay here and continue your earthly experience.

The second time, I was about 11 years old, and Vic was 16. Again, we were swimming in the river, at the old swimming hole. This was before the dam and beach were built in St. Malo Provincial Park. I was never a strong swimmer and could not make it across the river, panicked and started to go under. Vic was nearby with his girlfriend Aline. He jumped in fully clothed, and pulled me out of the deep end.

The third time was a year later. I almost drowned that third time and Vic marched me home and insisted that mom enroll me in swimming classes, as he had decided to join the Air Force and he would be leaving as soon as he turned 18 year old.

I took two years of swimming instructions and just hated it. The fear of drowning never left me. To this day, I am very respectful of large bodies of water and prefer to swim in a swimming pool where I know the depth of the water. Otherwise, even being on a boat leaves me with a very uneasy feeling. I probably drowned in another lifetime.

(I will have to find out, somehow.)

After he left, I asked the Universe for help. Instead of resisting the memories, I embraced both my weaknesses and my strengths through them. I reviewed, with compassion, all the ways I had violated myself for the sake of compromise, by not acknowledging myself in any way. I looked at all the places where I had literally sold my soul out of fear. It's only when our pain and disappointments are examined that they can be used as learning tools; then they impart life lessons. Most often, we don't even realize that all of our pain has a purpose. It is here to teach us, guide us, and give us the wisdom we need to deliver our gifts to the world.

All of us have gifts to share with the world, to contribute in a way that only our uniqueness allows. No one really knows what experiences we need in order that we may give our greatest gift, or when this gift will be called to action. Most of us repeatedly choose the comfort of what we know, staying inside our limited realities, just so we don't have to face the terror of that which we don't know. Many of us live by the saying, "Better the devil you know than the devil you don't know."

However, brewing beneath the surface is a deep dissatisfaction. Deep inside us is a "knowingness" that we need something else. This discontent is always pushing us, whispering in our ears, "There has to be more than this." That is where the struggle begins. We must uncover our pain and embrace it in order to heal our wounds and make peace with the past. We need to come to terms with who we are and why we are here. Unless we understand the tremendous lessons that life is teaching us, we will remain trapped inside the smallness of our minds.

I was now living a life that was allowing me to feel worthy and deserving of expressing the highest truth about myself. This whole episode with John's letter forced me to take responsibility for my reality - no matter what my ex-husband or anyone else was doing.

What resists, persists. I took the time to examine my entire human experience to that point – to embrace all the traumas, failures, challenges, and circumstances that life had thrown my way – and say, "Thank you, God, for giving me that experience. It forced me to take the high road and ask, "How am I going to grow from this moment on?"

Instead of denying the pain that I was going through, I used it for the purpose for which it was intended - to extract the wisdom from these experiences so that I could one day bring to others the gifts that only I possessed.

ALL OF ME IS MINE

If I'm still alone by now, it's by design
I only own myself, but all of me is mine.
But it's hard sometimes when strangers
Offer you a dime.
I only own myself, but all of me is mine.
If I still drink water when some folks drink wine
I only own myself, but all of me is mine.
But it's hard when city windows dance
With candleshine.
I only own myself, but all of me is mine.
The price you pay for sunshine
Can sometimes be quite dear
When all you have to sell is youth
It's hard to lose another year
My only forced submission
Has been the rape of time.
I only own myself, but all of me is mine.

Ron McKuen

CHAPTER 9

The Fall's Magic

September 1996

I actually had time by myself that fall, to reflect on how the past years had been about rediscovering my "self." I was learning to laugh and love life again. I was allowing myself to be happy.

It was a huge growth time for me - through meeting new friends, visiting new places, letting go of old pains, hurts, and people. There is a saying: "There's a reason why people from your past aren't in your future." Somehow, this was a comfort to me, as I allowed the different people to come and go through my life, touching me briefly through the experiences we shared together, and then walking away when the learning was done.

It had been a whole year since I had left John. In looking back, I could not believe how much I had changed in that year. I had rediscovered who I was, all by myself. I was independent, making my own decisions. I could buy what I wanted, when I wanted, paying whatever I wanted, without worrying about what "others" would say. What a liberating experience.

It was the first time in my life that I was responsible only for me (and Sammy, my bird, of course). I could read when I wanted to, listen to whatever music I wanted to, come, and go as I pleased, do some sewing in the middle of the night if I wanted to, invite people over, and entertain when, and how I pleased. What pleasure! What fun! How liberating!

I might have gone overboard in the entertainment department...it had been a pretty steady stream of people coming and going. Some weeks it felt as if I had a revolving door but I wasn't complaining. Before leaving, they had presented me with a guest book, which is still in use today entitled "Hotel Estelle."

 During that fall, my colleague and friend Kim Bogart and I would frequently drive out to the mountains. We were both on a "spiritual discovery" journey. We had been reading the same books, going to same courses, and being very open to new ways of thinking and to new experiences.

Melody, Kim, and I went to a concert in the Rockies "Mozart in the Mountains," in September of '96. It was incredible. The sound echoing off the mountains was amazing. What a great day.

Melody Jones was there to help guide us throughout this period of our lives and it was truly magical. I had been working with my

spirit guides constantly, and the more I asked, the more I started to receive. The more books I read, the more I wanted to learn.

This was such a period of growth for me. Calgary is a city of action - a city that offers its residents excitement, through a hub of activity and growth. Physically, I had bought a bicycle and was biking around Calgary. Mentally, I was taking evening management courses at the University of Calgary. Spiritually, I had taken courses with Melody, and through psychic readings. I was starting to figure out that I had been living my life unconsciously, to this point.

I realized that you could actually ask and be open to guidance, and that the answers would come, once you figured out what questions to ask.

I started asking my spirit guides to show me what it was I needed to do in this lifetime. I had a great job. I worked for CUMIS - an excellent caring company. It brought a certain amount of satisfaction, working in the co-operative, and credit union field, but I felt that somehow there was something more meant for me. I did not know what, or where, or how, but I started asking God to send me the people who would guide me to where I needed to go.

Through Cameron, I met Maureen Gannon, who pointed me to this phenomenal psychic named Erika. These are the notes from that psychic reading (December 4, 1996).

"Your friend Frank in Ottawa...he's a good business man. He has had difficulties in love life; he cannot make up his mind. He cannot commit, his mind controls over his heart. He is scared. He will run away, he loves you, but he feels trapped and cannot get away. Let him go, it will not go anywhere. Frank will be in your life for three years. You are smart...he needs you more than you need him.

Frank has a gift of talking that reaches people's hearts. He is a good counselor on a one-on-one basis. He is very objective, does not allow personal feelings in. However, he reaches people's hearts. In a few years, he will make more money. He feels he is too old to get back into the work force. He has a diploma missing. He needs to go back to school to get what is missing. He is very smart. He can do it. He has many opportunities to succeed. He is stuck in his present situation, with no way out. He is scared to organize or plan his life. I see him visiting you, but he will not stay. He is going to say hi/good bye.

For 1997...big changes for you. Your divorce is going to be final in 1997. For a first few months...nothing, then you will get into a new relationship. You are not going to get married right away. You will get a proposal, much later...years down the road.

Cameron is easygoing, easy making friends. He is very intelligent, more emotional/expressive, more heart over mind. This is better for you, more benefits/soul connection. He loves you/ compliments you. He is very "spiritual." This is a more relaxed relationship, filled with compromises. There will be no break-up; he is leaving the country. He would love to ask you to wait for him, but he will not ask. You are going to phone and keep in touch. He will come back after two years to make sure you are ok and you will have met someone else by then.

Cameron has a good future, not rich...he is too giving. He has many broken relationships. He gives his last dollar, good heart. He is artistic, has positive vibes. He feels happy with his decision to leave the country. He will never get married. He is a free spirit...too much to do, no time for permanent relationships. You are the one closest to his dreams, a very compromising person (you). He does not want to lose you as a friend. He likes his life. He is happy with what he has and what he can give, there are no regrets, he does not miss anything, and he is happy not chasing money. He is a good teacher of life...what is important and what is not important. He is very developed, ahead of us; he was in our shoes already. He is an old soul, does not need "stuff"...he has grown beyond this. His giving nature, spiritual connection, strong guardian angel, so he can let go, he has no need for treasures.

Estelle you will have a long life. You will overcome sickness...you were sick early in life. You are good in business/not good in love but you will grow wings. You are very sensitive, not just businessperson. You will meet someone else next year, around a celebration event. He is life-experienced, older, looks good...but read between the lines...please wait for "the One"...he is not it.

You are quite lucky. You can bring past to future, through the man you will meet. This man will commit and buy a ring. You have a gift...your gift is public speaking/good teacher...you will do that later. You will spend many years alone, and then you will meet someone. He loves you. You will be scared to commit, but its time to forget the past and commit to a future.

Your son, Marc, tell him not to change jobs now. Build family now. Just go to work and go home. Self-employment will come. He needs a job with a secure paycheck. It is a good partnership... good combo, those two. Do not be afraid for him. Luck is on his side. Tell him to wait at least a year. Keep one job and build up the other. Wait two years, and then move to own business. See little boy...two children, actually. They have a good future, moving/buying another house. He feels stuck, but change not recommended yet. He will get an offer from another company, a small company.

Wow, I had a lot of thinking to do. I continued seeking knowledge, and my best friend Suzanne would constantly suggest other books to read, and other ways to look at situations. She is a great listener and as I talked to her, I came to understand that there were many things that needed letting go.

My dear friend Melody arrived in December to cheer me up. It was my first official Christmas away from family and friends. We picked up a real Christmas tree (as opposed to an artificial one). We decorated it and had a wonderful Christmas dinner with Suzanne. The three of us were there for each other, at a time of year where being single is often very lonely.

PART III

A Year of Adventures

(1997)

ABSOLUTES

There are wild roses
That have bloomed
Far into December,
Seemingly without a reason.

And some faithful trees
Stay barren all year long.

Proving, I suppose,
The only thing consistent
Is inconsistency.

Rod McKuen

CHAPTER 10

New Experiences

January 1997

Dan and Russ stayed with me until January, when they found a nice two-bedroom suite to rent, not too far away from me. I was sad to see them go but understood their need for independence.

To cheer me up after my two nephews moved out, Cameron suggested we drive up to Jasper for some downhill skiing. I was not a skier yet, but decided that if I was going to be living close to the mountains, I had better learn how. When we arrived in Jasper, I immediately booked a woman skiing instructor for the entire day. She was wonderful, patient and kind.

She showed me how to plow the skis...put on the brakes, that is. Once I had mastered how to stop anytime, we jumped on the ski lift and went up to the top of the mountain. I was petrified. I did not know how to get off the ski lift and her first attempt to get me off with her while the ski lift was still moving...well, we both wound up tumbling off to the side. She got up, laughing, and said: "Well, that's the worst you'll ever have to face…getting off the ski lift." It took us two hours to get down the mountain the first time. She would ski about fifteen feet ahead of me, stop, turn around, and then I would ski to her. She said if I could not stop, that she would be there to stop me, and she did. Amazingly, I gained confidence very quickly.

The second time, when I went up the ski lift, I tumbled off it by myself. I did not want to drag her with me. However, I got out of the way of the ski lift, picked myself up, and decided it appeared that I was "ski-lift challenged." I was determined to conquer that as well.

At noon, when we stopped for lunch, we met up with Cameron who had been downhill skiing the black runs all morning. He asked how the lessons were progressing, and I was very pleased to report that I had done two whole runs!

On our drive back to Calgary, through the ice fields, we stopped to admire some mountain climbers who were rappelling down the sheer side of a mountain; it was truly amazing to watch.

I immediately told Cameron, "Don't even think about it. That is something I know I'll never do." I declared emphatically. I returned to Calgary a novice ski lift challenged skier but, hey, it was a beginning! I could not believe I had actually done it.

In February, I had a long telephone conversation with Frank, (from Ottawa). He had met another woman and we agreed that our association needed to end, so that he could move on. I was sad that Frank wanted to end our friendship. It is hard to say goodbye to someone who was there to see you through a rough part of your life. We had talked about it many times before, that the time would come when we would go on our own paths separately. I was scared that I would not have him to lean on anymore. He was right. I had become too dependent on him as a counselor and it was time to break the ties and move on, for both of us.

As I reflected on the fact that I shall never see him again, I felt regret at the lost potential of a great relationship that could have developed, given a chance. Strangely enough, when you love someone enough, you can let him or her go.

I was starting to see the lesson in this for me, as I saw now what John must have been going through and why he had such a hart time in letting go of the past. This must have been torture for him. I prayed: "Help me deal fairly with him, in order to be able to face him when our grandchild is born. Give me the courage to face what I must."

March 1997

Our long-awaited free trip finally arrived, and Monique and I went to Cuba. We talked about what we might bring, and discussed how poor people were there. We brought clothes, jewelry, toys, medicine…anything we could think of that they might not have there.

Our first morning in Cuba at our resort, we were excited. We decide to make two stacks on our pillows, with a letter to our house cleaner (whoever she might be), detailing all that we were giving her that day. We signed it with our name, address and resort number, so that she would not be accused of stealing, or have to worry about it.

We left for the day. When we returned to our resort later in the day, there was this petite, cute little house cleaner (in her late twenties) pacing up and down in front of our door. She pointed to the door number and pointed at us: "Les signoras?"

We replied, "Si!" We all smiled foolishly at each other. She did not speak English at all and we had a very limited command of Spanish, so we gestured a lot. Her name was Belkis Dominiquez Almaquer. She kept holding her face with her hands, shaking it back and forth, and saying, "Oh, les signoras...muchos gracias!"

Every day, we did the same thing…another pile of stuff would be prepared for her. We found out she had a 9-year old son. Luckily, we had brought pencils, notebooks, stickers and generic toys and candies for children. When we left at the end of the week, we left a twenty-dollar bill for her. We found out that she only made five dollars per month. Wow! Talk about a reality check!

After coming back home, we corresponded with her. I tried to send her things, but she never got them, so reverted to just sending postcards. That, at least, she received. Any packages sent were opened by the post office workers, the contents taken and the letters thrown away. It was very disheartening, as we could not send anything that would find its way to her.

I finally faxed her at the Resort, asking her to fax me a bank account where I could send her money. She faxed me back the information. It cost me over one hundred dollars to send her one hundred and fifty dollars. That was very discouraging as well. She faxed me back that she had received the money and that was the last time I heard from her. I don't know if someone confiscated the money or what, but all efforts to communicate with her were fruitless thereafter.

That will not stop me from making other random acts of

kindness wherever I go, and I have learned that it is okay to just give, without expectations   Just give with the best of intentions for the good and benefit of all, and then let go of the outcome… let it go!

April 1997

Cameron left for Korea. It threw me for a loop. I had really relied on his friendship. I did not realize how much it would hurt to see him go. I felt the darkness closing in on me again and I was scared. I did not want to go out. I pulled back into myself.

Maureen had told me jokingly prior to Cameron's leaving: "Oh no! I'll have to look after you, once Cameron's gone to Korea." I vowed to myself that would not happen. I refused to lean on anyone. Whenever she would phone, I never complained or cried, but she could hear it in my voice, that I was having low moments.

However, spring was in the air and it was hard to stay down for long. After all, I had gone through so much in such short a time, and look at the transformation that had happened in my life in a short span of twenty months.

I had met so many good people on this leg of the journey… people I could rely on for friendship, encouragement, support, and love. What else could one ask for? I found that when I looked in the mirror, I saw someone I recognized now. I remembered those little pieces of myself that I had given away one by one, which seemed so insignificant at the time and I wondered what had become of me. I remembered experiencing the feeling of disappearing before my very eyes. I sure had not planned it that way; it just seemed to happen over the years.

Where just to stay alive, to say nothing of staying on top, seemed to require conflicting attitudes - if you were a successful person, you had to keep going in the rat race to stay there; if you were poor, you had to keep going to survive. If you didn't, you had the impression that it would not be long before you would fall behind.

There was never any time for just yourself, to do nothing, to enjoy a sunset, to listen to a bird sing, to watch a bee bumble, to hear what you were thinking, much less what anybody else was thinking.

More and more, as I read and thought, I was forced to reexamine motives, to rethink, or perhaps to think for the first time, about values and aspects of living I had previously simply accepted. I had been used to living in a world where it was nearly impossible to take the time to look inside yourself.

Human contact seemed superficial, striving for meaningful goals, wanting deeper meaning but only talking around it. Competitive living left no time for what we were, who we could be, and what we could mean to each other. I had seen very few relationships with real and lasting meaning...my own included.

Instead of going deeper, we chose to respond to urges to be comfortable, to accept the limits and restrictions imposed by safe superficiality, to be successful and well-attended creatures of comfort with protection and warmth.

Over the past 20 months, I had been challenged by my fear of the unknown - challenges from what more I could be or was, challenges from what more I could understand and how that might threaten me.

However, I had faced my biggest challenge…what it meant to end up alone. Alone…there was that word that had haunted me for years. Everyone was afraid of being alone. Yet, it did not really matter who we lived with or slept with or loved or married. In the final analysis, we were all alone…alone with ourselves…and that is where the rub came. So many relationships were failing because the people involved did not know whom they were, much less the person or people with whom they were involved.

I thought that was now changing. People were now beginning to search into their own depths as a kind of instinctive survival mechanism to offset the polarity of violence and disturbance that was clearly stalking the world. People were accepting their worthiness and finding the potential for unbridled joy in themselves. It could be that thousands of people all over the world were involved with this mystery, of whether or not there was a life beyond the physical.

I wondered what my other friends who were not into reading and thinking what I was reading and thinking… anything of a spiritual nature…would it embarrass them, or would they think I was "really losing it"…given the kind of world we live in. But all the books I was reading…Deepak Chopra, Sylvia Browne, Edward Cayce, Doreen Virtue, Caroline Myss, Gary Zukav… they were all saying the same thing.

It was in the comfort and the magic of books, my companions in life since I had first learned to read, that I found solace and wisdom as I turned to them once again. They helped me go within and open myself to learning anew.

FAITH

Since all that is was ever bound to be;
Since grim, eternal laws our Being bind;
And both the riddle and the answer find,
And both the carnage and the calm decree;
Since plain within the Book of Destiny
Is written all the journey of mankind
Inexorably to the end; since blind
And mortal puppets playing parts are we:

Then let's have faith; good cometh out of ill;
The power that shaped the strife shall end the strife;
Then let's bow down before the Unknown Will;
Fight on, believing all is well with life;
Seeing within the worst of War's red rage
The gleam, the glory of the Golden Age.

Robert William Service

CHAPTER 11

Psychic Messages

May 1997

My assistant Lynne Cruikshank came up to me. "I need to talk to you right away," she insisted. I immediately ushered into my office and closed the door.

"What's up?" I asked.

"You'll maybe think I'm crazy, but I went to see a medium (psychic) last night. Her name is Marguerite Davenport and she told me that you were moving somewhere else," she blurted out. I was stunned. She and I had a very close business and personal relationship. We really liked working together and got along famously.

I quickly reassured her that I had absolutely no intentions of moving anywhere.

She replied, "Well, she said that it would be something out of your control, but that you would be leaving Calgary."

"Well, if it is meant to be, so be it. I guess we will just have to wait and see what develops." We hugged and both went back to work, in a very thoughtful state.

Her medium was an exceptional person, I knew, as Suzanne had also been to see her, and she had been incredibly accurate about her predictions. I pondered this information, wondering what could possibly be coming up for me and where this move would take me.

I decided not to worry and to leave it up to God. I asked God, "As long as this move takes me in the right direction, in the direction of the path you want me on, bring it on. Thy will be done!" I remembered the teachings from "Feel the Fear and Do It Anyways"…instead of fighting it, surrender to it. After that, I quickly forgot about it, and went on with my life.

Then, a few weeks later, I literally ran into this woman, who also turned out to be a psychic. I invited her over to the condominium for a reading. These are excerpts from that May 1997 psychic reading with Helen Randle:

"Past: seven years in transformation, provided growth opportunities, transition period.

Present: well respected, people look to you for advice, admired.

Future: spiritual man/ healing man loves you, sees you as golden chalice. You have been in a tunnel/cave recently. You are just coming out of it now, with new insights.

Future: Your son Marc and his family will be near you. You

will be moving. New job, lots of money. You are a giver. Someone needs your guidance and money… you need to help him. You will be prosperous in your new career.

You are going to be with your mate, a spiritual man, who is also on a spiritual journey, you will be together…not yet, but you have to wait for him, quite a long time, but he's worth the wait.

You have a seventh angel who will show up in the near future. She has held back until your feminine side balances out. You will be growing spiritually; psychic abilities will come through. Do not agonize. What you must do will come to you effortlessly. Let it happen. You have a high priestess in your life, someone who guides/heals you. You are very connected."

I thanked her so very much for that burst of insight. I so needed to hear those messages. That night, I asked my angel guides, "Send me guidance, love, protect me, and help me grow spiritually and psychically."

Now, some of you may ask, "What is the difference between a psychic and a medium?" Mainly, the word psychic refers to an ability to perceive information hidden from the normal senses through what is described as extrasensory perception, or to those people said to have such abilities

Psychics appear regularly in fiction and science fiction, such as The Dead Zone by Stephen King. Psychics provide advice and counsel to clients. Some famous contemporary psychics include Sylvia Browne, and John Edward. Most psychics do not communicate with the spirit world. Their gifts are based purely on the physical level. Usually, they counsel people with present situations, but will not provide information on a person's past. They do not discuss anything about spirit beings, or bring messages from them.

On the other hand, mediums are instruments of spirit connections. They bring messages from the spirit world regarding past, present and future events. Mediums focus on giving proof of survival. They are able to connect with loved ones who have transitioned over to the other side and give you messages from them – messages that are meaningful only for you. An example would be when someone from the other side gives you the message where to find a certain item, such as a lost ring. This is concrete proof of survival.

Mediums do not predict future events (fortune telling), and deal with more spiritual matters than, "When will I meet the man of my dreams?" However, they can and do provide guidance in the area of relationships. Readings with mediums can provide you with knowledge about your spirit guides (names, physical features and what they are here to help you with) and lead you to new insights on your spirituality.

When you feel it's time for a reading, write down the information you are seeking before deciding if you should look for a psychic or a medium.

May 1997

In May, Leslie came out from Winnipeg for a short visit. She insisted that we stay in and have a relaxing long-weekend together...no driving anywhere, no visiting anything. "Estelle," she lectured me, with concern: "I've never seen you this stressed out and drained. You've lost weight (which was a good thing, I thought), but you're working too much."

"You're right. I replied. "I figured it out that I've spent 77 days in airports in the past twelve months." We relaxed, drank a little Scotch, listened to some Blues at the "King Eddy," and watched some marathon movies on TV.

She gave me the long road of life speech: "You have to look after yourself. You need to make yourself number one; otherwise you're no good to anyone at all."

I agreed. I could see that she was correct in her analysis. She gave me the example of a car: You have a car, you look after it, make sure it has enough gas and oil. When it is low on gas, you stop and refuel. Take that analogy, and transfer it to your body. When it is low on energy, you have to stop. You need to take care of yourself. Take time out to re-energize; otherwise, you will burn out.

It made a lot of sense to me. I vowed to change my habits, to take time out when my energy was low. I started going out to the mountains to meditate and absorb their energy. I would go hug a tree to accept their energy (which they gladly give you, free of charge…go ahead, and try it. It works…you will see!).

Weeks later, when Maureen phoned, I told her, "Well, I must be feeling better. I painted my toenails today. The first time since Cameron left!" I was elated, and so was she. She drove over and personally delivered a fresh bouquet of flowers in celebration. We became close friends from that moment on, to this day.

To celebrate further, we drove out to Banff. Maureen had booked us for a Swedish massage at the Banff School of Arts, with Kate Kiss. Kate was a blonde-haired Swede, in her late sixties, but looked forty. She had energy, enthusiasm, and strong healing hands.

I did not know Kate and had never been to the Banff School of Art. While driving out to Banff, Maureen told me that Kate had psychic abilities and that I should not be surprised at whatever she would have to say. I undressed and lay down on the massage table.

Kate walked in, touched my foot in passing, and said, "Get the dog! You want a dog and you are denying yourself one. You think you are traveling too much and that you will have no one to take care of it. There is a dog waiting for you at the SPCA. Go there once a week, until the dog comes to you. Your neighbors and friends will all want to take care of your dog, so get the dog."

Well, I was flabbergasted. I had not told anyone of my secret desire to get a dog. I had missed having a dog around terribly, since Marc, Lizanne had gotten married, and Skip had gone to live with them. Kate's message left me elated. I was walking on air when I left Banff that day. Every week after that, for about three months, I went to the local SPCA to visit the dogs. Of course, I loved and wanted to adopt them all. I would sign up for adoption, and others ahead of me would get the dog. I was not discouraged. I knew there was a dog that would one day be there for me.

FRIENDSHIP OATH

"By accepting the responsibility of being your friend,
I promise to be honest and trustworthy.
I will try to work out any differences or conflicts that we may have and put the time and effort into our friendship that it requires.
I know we both have work (or school), family, and personal obligations, and we will respect each other's other relationships and commitments, but I will also be committed to this friendship.
I will try to only give advice if it's asked and I will also try to be your friend, unconditionally. I will keep your confidences. However, I will also share with you if it is my policy to never keep anything from my spouse or any other primary relationship, with whom I entrust all my secrets.
I will try to remember your birthday and be there for you when times are tough and when times are grand. Making time to talk, communicate by mail or e-mail, or getting together is a priority. I will celebrate your achievements even though I know a tiny bit of envy or competitiveness is normal. I will bring fun and joy to your life as much as I am able to as I cherish our past, present, and future friendship."

Dr. Jan Yager

CHAPTER 12

The Importance of Friendships

June 1997

Kathy Hammond came out for a two-week holiday. Her visit coincided with the World Police and Firemen Games being held in Calgary that week. We met some singles from Australia, Italy, and San Juan.

It was so much fun. Albino, (coach) and Walter (interpreter), and Fosco (bench-press) were firefighters from Italy, in the bench-pressing competition (for which Fosco won a medal), so we agreed to go and watch their events. Kathy and I went out to buy some Italian-English dictionaries, so that we could communicate with them when the interpreter was not around. It really got hilarious at times.

On Wednesday of that week, the Italians had a day off, so we offered to take them into the mountains, which they gratefully accepted. They had never been to Canada, so it was our patriotic duty to show them the incredible Rocky Mountains.

We drove into Kannanaskis Country, rented some bikes, and drove around all afternoon in the mountain trails. Albino kept saying, "Bellissimo!" We agreed. That night, we invited them back to the condominium, and invited our neighbors to join us for a "Western Hospitality BBQ steak dinner." It was a real hit – one of those "random acts of kindness" that warms the heart.

After they left on Friday, to return to Italy, Kathy and I took a well-deserved rest.

The next day, we drove out to Spruce Meadows to watch some horse jumping competitions. It was nice and relaxing, after that exhausting week.

Another friend from Ontario came out that same week... Steve Lambert.

Steve and I had worked together for over ten years Steve worked at our Head Office in Burlington, and was the Vice-President, Marketing Division.

We would work often together, and had developed a mutual respect for each other's skills. Steve is an out-of-the-box thinker with very innovative ideas, filled with enthusiasm and a great sense of humor. We got along great, professionally and became good friends as well.

When I had phoned him to let him know that John and I were getting a divorce, he was full of compassion and caring. He questioned my decision, saying: "You know how much pain you'll be going through? Well, multiply it by twenty. That is how bad it is going to get. Are you absolutely sure you want to go through that? That you're strong enough to go it alone?" He explained his comments were based on his personal experience, on the rough time he went through with his first marriage, which had lasted less than a year, when he was in his early twenties.

He was out west going to interviews. He and his second wife Debbie and their two daughters wanted to relocate out west, as Debbie was originally from Edmonton. Because Kathy was already installed in the guest room, Steve wound up sleeping on the hide-a bed, which I had just purchased for the living room.

The first morning Steve got up and he complained he had spring marks on his butt. We laughed so hard; especially when we looked at the mattress and found that it had been laid with the springs up instead of down. We quickly corrected that but made him give us a morning butt report for the rest of his stay.

A few nights later, Steve insisted on cooking a gourmet meal for his "soul sisters" (Suzanne, Kathy, and me). He was a marvelous cook and as long as we acted as the "sous-chef," he controlled the entire orchestration of this wonderful meal.

After the meal, Kathy said, "I was in the bathroom of the saloon last night, and bought each of you a present." Well, we burst out laughing. What kind of present do you get in a public bathroom? Now I know what you are thinking, 'because we were thinking the same thing...condoms, right? Wrong!

Tattoos! She had bought us some disposable Mickey Mouse cartoon character tattoos. They only last as long as your next shower, thank you!

Everyone went to a different room to put their tattoo somewhere on their body and when we got back to the dining room, we had to guess where. We had a great time guessing. The first one up was Suzanne. She is conservative, so I guessed on her arm and I was right. The next one was Steve. You guess! On his butt, right? Right! That was too obvious after the teasing that had gone on all week. Then, Kathy was harder to guess. She can be crazy… who would have guessed on her arm! I sure did not.

After everyone left, I reflected deeply on friendships – those that I had left behind in Manitoba and the new friendships that I had been blessed with making since moving to Calgary. Friends – I vowed I would never underestimate their value. You know you have a friend for life when you can't sleep and have a lot on your mind, and they don't mind talking about nothing to get your mind off everything.

You know you have a friend for life when something is wrong and they know it just by the look in their eyes, and that unspoken communication says it all. Sometimes, just at the tone of my voice, Suzanne would instantly pick up that I was going through a tough time. She would show up at the door with a bottle of wine, and a good book for me to get inspiration from and we would talk for hours, until my spirits had lifted.

Friends – they can make you laugh when skies are the darkest, and they're there with a good movie and some popcorn when you're totally depressed. And even if you're a thousand miles apart, it doesn't matter because what you share with this friend is so much deeper than what lies on top that distance plays no role in your friendship. Kathy was such a friend. She lived thousands of miles away, but that didn't matter. She would call me and we would chat for hours in the evening. You may have thought that your need to chat was a waste of time, but it's really a natural female quality in connecting with others.

Kathy was the most upbeat person I had ever met in my life.

She showed such caring for her friends and I was blessed to count myself as one of them. Kathy worked out of the CUMIS Head Office in Burlington, Ontario. I was doubly blessed, as we had both a working relationship and a friendship.

After I left John, she was always checking up on me to make sure that I was coping on my own. She spent many of her holidays with me and I so appreciated that. Kathy knew when to push me when I needed it, but never too hard. She knew when to stand back when the time was right but never too far.

I had felt unable to deepen my relationship with my women-friends while I had been married to John. He frowned upon my being friends with single women, and the repercussions of going against his wishes weren't conducive to my pushing that issue and so I didn't.

Of course, you only allow what happens to yourself. But I was never a fighter. I always believed that the truth and the intentions coming from the heart were good enough. By accepting these limitations, I missed accessing the knowledge and wisdom of those women who could have been more than "ships that pass in the night".

We women need daily connection with others who are on a similar journey, with whom we have a sense of history and vision. We need to share our lives with others, to discuss our problems, to nurture each other, and to acknowledge that our feminine strengths form the path to a fulfilled life.

My life was so much better because I knew them and they brought out the best in me. I treasured my friendships and I vowed to be a friend that a friend would like to have. I asked my Angel of Friendship – Frouglishyn to assist me in making conscious choices by keeping myself open to new introductions and new friends and to strengthen the bonds of friendship in this community of like-minded souls, who were my women-friends.

I Mark Your Courage

I had no profound feelings of shock or surprise
to those matter-of-fact revelations
which spelled the end of this chapter of your life.

It was, as you put it, too late for recriminations,
and the horrendous realities could be no worse
for having faced them.

Ivan Donn Carswell

CHAPTER 13

Psychic Reading with Erika

August 1997

One night, Maureen had made an appointment for both of us with her psychic Erika. As soon as I walked in the door, Erika said, "Where are you moving to? I see a moving van behind you!"

Well, I was stunned. There it was, a second time, from a different psychic. I replied, "I don't know…you tell me!" Then, she went on to give me the following reading: Here are some excerpts from that reading in Calgary.

"You are moving to Winnipeg, you will get the house that you want, at the price you want. It is a good house. You will be happy there. You will meet a man in that city. You will be close and happy. He is a nice man. You will get married again…but not soon.

"Cameron - don't wait for him. Have another relationship. He will stay overseas for many years. He will come back to see if you are free. You will have met someone else by then.

"Frank... really got burned in his last relationship. He is smart, well balanced. He will always choose mind over heart. He will never get married. He wants no commitments. He has feelings for you. You will have to go to Ottawa if you want him. You are welcome there. You would have a good life together.

"Business...change coming. Things will change drastically. It is good for you. You will have an opportunity to apply for another job with a different company. It would mean more money, with a steady, good income. You may not take it.

"Career...many changes through 1998. It will be a very hectic time - very stressful, but nice stress. You are moving to a different career, change will be better for you. Be patient. There's a new direction coming slowly but strong – with many opportunities and new ideas – something completely different, but very good. Don't lose trust and belief. You are very gifted with people. You will find new clientele and be very good at it.

"There is a new man coming into your life...not yet, but wait for him. He will be in the same city as you. He is handsome, with hazel eyes. He has been married before, two sons. You will be married again...many years down the road. You need to learn to share again. You need to learn to share intimate part. You do not share bathroom. Chin up... commit to this new man. You will know it is he when you do not mind sharing a bathroom and when you start making room for him in your bedroom. Much later, you will be buying a new house together. He is a very calm man. He will offer you a ring. You will grow old with this man by your side. You will have a nice house, with a nice man.

"Your health...there is a problem in your chest...something with your lungs. There are stomach problems. Not serious, but needs attention.

She said, "Well, you're also going to meet a man soon, here in Calgary...a man with two dogs. However, he is not the one you are going to marry. The man you're going to marry will be in the same city that you're moving to." You will be buying a house...you will know it is the right one, something will resonate within you when you walk in. It will be at the right time, at the right price for you."

The rest of her reading was a blur. All I could think was - I guess I am moving away. I meditated after I got back home, and asked God, "Whatever or wherever I'm going, let it be for the good and benefit of all what cross my path." Then I released it to the Universe.

KINDRED SPIRITS[4]

"Animals are a gift to the human race –
A gift that humans rarely take full advantage of.
Only now are we even beginning
To understand what a marvelous blessing
Animals truly are."

Allen M. Schoen, Author

---

[4] How the Remarkable Bond between Humans and Animals Can Change the Way we Life. Allen M. Schoen, D.V.M., M.S., is one of the most sought-after doctors of veterinary medicine in the nation. He has also written: Love, Miracles, and Animal Healing. For more information, go to   Kindred Spirits will touch and enlighten anyone seeking deeper levels of awareness and uplifting stories of true love.

CHAPTER 14

Getting a Shadow

August 1997

Sure enough, during my weekly visits to the SPCA, there was this black American Cocker Spaniel, a two-year-old male, who had just been brought it. He was found on the street. He had a dog tag that said his name was "Bear" with a phone number but there was no answer at the residence and they were unable to track down his owners. He was ten pounds under weight, had an ear and an eye infection, and had to be neutered (adoption rules). I loved him instantly. He needed me and I needed him more. I adopted him immediately.

I was walking around the room and he started to follow me around so, of course, I named him "Shadow." He had to go to the vet's for a few days before I could bring him home. Poor little guy. He was so sick. I took a week of holidays to help him settle into his new home.

My girlfriend Sue and her husband Bert and their two daughters came out from Winnipeg for a one-week stay, arriving the day I brought Shadow home. Sue had a little male Pomeranian dog "Simba," so Shadow had some company while we went out sight-seeing, and splashing around at the water park.

After one week of getting him used to Sammy, the condo, and me, I had to go back to work. There were workers replacing the roof that had been damaged during a severe hailstorm a few weeks earlier, so as I left, I warned them that I had a new dog and this was his first day alone, so they might hear some howling.

I quickly hurried home early afternoon, and the workers told me that he had howled for about six hours. When I opened the door, he fell into my arms, and a tiny squeak came out…he had no sound left. I held him, cried with him, and reassured him that I would never leave him; but that I had to go to work, every day and he would have to be brave and learn to guard the condominium and Sammy.

The next day, the workers reported that he had only howled for four hours - the third day only two hours and the fourth day fifteen minutes. By Friday of the first week home alone, Shadow was resigned and accepted the fact that I would leave him during the day. When I came home, I would grab the leash and away we would go for a long walk down into the dog park, where I would let him go in the "off leash" area. However, he stuck to me like a Shadow! He has never run off to check out the other dogs.

He brought me such pleasure. I loved walking in at night and be greeted by a wagging tail and a lick on the face, and Sammy chirping. It felt wonderful to have a four-legged friend, as well as a feathered friend. I brought him for a grooming and did not recognize him when I picked him up. He cleaned up pretty good. He now looked like this:

At the end of September, the Garage Sale Guru competition ended and Karen won on the last weekend with an additional three brass animals, to win by two. I was humble in defeat and she was bragging all over the condominium corporation about her wins. The challenge had been that the loser would prepare a seven-course meal for the winner.

I threatened that my seven-course meal would be a hot dog and a six-pack of beer. However, in the meantime, I was

Getting a Shadow   139

preparing a luscious evening celebration, and hand-delivered their invitation.

We drank champagne and toasted Karen, our Garage Sale Guru.

The dinner celebration was a huge success, reliving our garage sale-ing finds and treasures. Life is full of opportunities to celebrate the "now" of life. This was such a time.

Thanksgiving came around, and Maureen invited me over for thanksgiving dinner. She had invited some other friends and when I walked in, a very nice Englishman, named Peter Saunders greeted me. We started talking and got along famously. He was a Commercial photographer.

He had started his career in photography in England and some of his famous work includes an early photo of The Beatles (before they were famous), as well as the photo credits of the TV show "The Avengers, with Emma Peel." I was impressed.

He insisted on driving me home that night and returned the next day to drive me back to Maureen to pick up my car. Then, he asked if I wanted to go and walk his two dogs with him by the Bow River.

I remembered what Erika, the psychic had said, and thought to myself: "Oh my…this is the man that I'm meant to meet here but not the one that I'll be marrying." Interesting!

We started going out on a regular basis, driving to the

mountains to just sit and stare at them, going to regional plays, and dining at his favorite – Antoinetta's Italian Restaurant. She greeted us like royalty whenever we went to dine there. Peter had photographed some of her dishes for her cookbook: "Antoinetta's Italian Cooking." He always saw things with an incredible photographic eye.

Peter always had his camera with him, and it was truly amazing to hang around with him. He took this picture on one of our trips to Kannanaskis Country. This is one of his photographs:

He loved Shadow, and we would take all three of our dogs for long walks on the hill overlooking Calgary. That was such a beautiful view of the city, with the Rocky Mountains in the background. Peter's dogs just accepted Shadow as if he had been around for years.

It was fun watching them run around chasing sticks. He took a picture of his two dogs, Grizzly and Licorice, with a stick between them. He named it:

"Good friends stick together."

He asked me if he could take pictures of Shadow to use as advertising for "Pawtraits" that people want done of their pets. My Shadow - a dog model.

THREADS OF A JOURNEY

A tapestry is being stitched
story by story,
step by step, thread by thread
Pictures of her life come alive
with threads of gold,
of silver, of royal purple,
of hope, of faith, of love
her story unfolding
in the fabric, the knitted
tapestry of her life

Raymond A. Foss

CHAPTER 15

Psychic Predictions Come True

October 1997

A few weeks later, I received an early morning call from my Vice-President in Burlington. "There have been some high-level decisions made that will affect your future. I'm flying out to meet with you immediately. I will be there by 2:00 pm. Pick me up at the airport, and let's have a late lunch together. I will tell you all about it. Don't let your staff know about this yet," he cautioned before he hung up.

I sat there, at my kitchen table, with Sammy on my shoulder and Shadow lying down at my feet and pondered my future. "This is it." I told myself. "I guess I'm moving somewhere. Do not be scared…do not let fear close you to new opportunities. Look where you have been so far. It has been a heck of a ride. Stay open to change and accept with love. This is where God wants you to go."

"Well, if I was being fired, he wouldn't be taking me out for lunch. This I know for sure," I told myself. I was a little uneasy, I will admit. "Change is never easy," I reminded myself. "Stay in the moment and put your love and trust in God." I kept repeating to myself as I drove to the airport that day.

I picked up my boss, Terry Pepler, and we made small talk from the airport to the restaurant. After ordering our lunch, I finally broke the silence: "Okay, Terry…what's up? Don't keep me in suspense any longer." I pleaded with him.

"Well, you may not like this, Estelle," he replied. "We've made some structural changes throughout Canada and this means that three Regional Manager Positions have been eliminated…yours is one of them."

Very calmly, I nodded and answered: "I've been getting messages all summer, that something was coming…I just didn't know what. I'm relieved to finally know."

"So," I continued, "what does this mean for me? If I was being fired, we wouldn't be having lunch…so, what do you have in mind?"

"You know me well," he replied. "I'm amazed, and relieved that you're taking this news so calmly." He continued: "You're right. We do have a few options for you to consider about your future. One option is for you to step down as Regional Manager, but continue as Senior Account Manager, either here in Calgary, or back in Winnipeg."

"That is where we really need you - in Winnipeg. Your long-time colleague, Fabien Desmarais, in retiring soon, and we would like you to go back to Winnipeg and take over his bilingual position as Senior Account Manager."

I must admit that I was shocked at that option. I had never envisioned myself going back home. I had thought that perhaps I would be offered a position at Head Office in Burlington, but not of going back to Winnipeg.

"Take your time to consider your options, Estelle." Terry continued. "I thought that with your family and your new grandson there, that you would seriously consider that your best option. However, if you want to stay in Calgary, that is also available to you. Take a few days off work, and really think this decision thoroughly. Call me by the end of the week to let me know your decision. In the meantime, let's keep this conversation to ourselves," he ended.

"No," I replied, "I've been told by higher powers that I'd be moving to another city…so I guess that my destiny is calling me home. It makes sense. My parents are getting older and I want to be close by for the remaining years that they have."

"You know how important family is to me, Terry." I continued. "And you're right…I want to be close to see my new grandson grow and be a part of his life, not just for a visit now and then, but accessible on an as-needed basis."" Enough time has passed to heal the wounds of the divorce and I'm much stronger now that I know who I am."

"Yes," I nodded emphatically. "I'm going home. The decision is made. It is official. I will not change my mind. You can put the wheels in motion to affect the move. Let me know the periods. I'll work with them." We shook hands on it and I drove him back to the airport.

Once I returned to my condominium, I phoned Lynne at the office. I had told her that I had an important meeting that day but had not told her with whom or why. As soon as she answered the phone, I told her: "Lynne, I have some news for you. Are you ready for this?

She said, "I know what you're going to say…you're leaving. Just like the psychic said, aren't you?"

"Yes, that's right!" I confirmed. "Thank you so much for preparing me for this all those months ago. I think it would have been a horrendous shock, had I not been advised by one psychic, through you, and another psychic, through Maureen, that this was coming."

"This move is going to be happening fairly quickly," I informed Lynne. "Probably over the next six to eight weeks. Please keep this information to yourself, for now. Can you call the staff together for an emergency meeting tomorrow morning?"

"Sure, no problem." Lynne replied. "I'll get on it right away. Are you going to be okay? Do you want someone to go over to be with you right now?" she inquired, concerned.

"No," I stated confidently. "I'll be just fine. I need time by myself to sort out exactly what this means, but I trust that this is the path that I'm meant to be on, so I'm moving forward."

My second phone call was to my son. "Marc!" I exclaimed, "Guess what? I'm moving back home, to Winnipeg."

"No way!" Marc replied. "How come? What's happening?"

I explained about the Company's restructuring plans and the two options that were on the table for me. "I think I'm ready to come home."

"With Mom and Dad getting older and with Mathew…I want to be there to enjoy him. So, I'm coming home." I confirmed happily.

The move happened quickly. I put the condominium for sale and it sold within days at a very handsome profit. As the psychic had predicted, I found a house that I could afford, in a very quiet neighborhood, very close to my son, and only a 40-minute drive to my parents place.

Suzanne and I spent the last days together, walking Shadow, and talking about where the journey was taking us. She was also moving back to Winnipeg, as soon as she was finished with her Masters in Counseling, so we talked about her moving in with me until she could find a condo close by. We did not want to lose the closeness that had developed between us.

My next-door neighbor Karen Lopston offered to drive back to Winnipeg with me, and Shadow and Sammy. We decided to drive straight through. Even though we drove through some fog, sleet, and some snow flurries, we managed to get to Marc's house by midnight, very exhausted.

Shadow had been simply marvelous. We would stop every two hours, and he would immediately jump out, go and do his business, drink a few sips of water, and jump back in, ready to move on. He was simply amazing.

The next day, the moving van came and, with their help, and Karen's help, within a few days, I was settled in my new house in Winnipeg, with Shadow and Sammy.

I sat down, took a deep breath and thought: "Well, it's November. Winter is coming and here I am, alone." I could never have imagined myself coming full circle back home so quickly. So much had happened to me in such a short period. I remember thinking how the events in our lives happen in a sequence in time, but in their significance to ourselves, they find their own order…the continuous thread of revelation.

Skeletons, that I believed were long-since buried, began to rattle their bones. I guess that I had not completely worked through all the old experiences and traumas. How disquieting when memories long hidden from consciousness signal us that they are ready to be worked through…again!

Can we believe that our own inner process knows when we are ready to deal with old issues? Can we trust that the very fact that they are coming up is an indication of how much we have grown and how strong we are? Can we trust that there is something within us that knows more than we know; and that trusting it, instead of fighting it, can only result in further healing?

I was home again, stronger and ready for whatever awaited me.

PART IV

The Spiritual Awakening

(1999)

A NOVEMBER DAISY

Afterthought of summer's bloom!
Late arrival at the feast,
Coming when the songs have ceased
And the merry guests departed,
Leaving but an empty room,
Silence, solitude, and gloom.
Are you lonely, heavy-hearted;
You, the last of all your kind,
Nodding in the autumn wind;
Now that all your friends are flown,
Blooming late and all alone?

Once the daisies gold and white
Sea-like through the meadow rolled:
Once my heart could hardly hold
All its pleasures. I remember,
In the flood of youth's delight
Separate joys were lost to sight.
That was summer! Now November
Sets the perfect flower apart;
Gives each blossom of the heart
Meaning, beauty, grace unknown, —
Blooming late and all alone.

Henry Van Dyke

CHAPTER 16

Destiny Calls Me Home

December 1997

Where Calgary had offered a youthful exuberance and vibrancy – a city of constant activity, growth and doing – Winnipeg represented stability, familiarity, and safety.

Many outsiders have tried to knock Winnipeg...calling it "Winter' peg, Loser' peg, or Mosquito' peg." However, to Winnipeggers, its Canada's best kept secret.

Beneath the deceptive quietness of the City lies a vortex of creativity. There is a huge artistic community, where the residents support their own. Winnipeg is a city of creativity and spirituality.

Part of me wanted to come home, I admit. I had missed being close to my family and friends. However, part of me wanted to run back to Calgary, where I had learned to know and love my self. I was determined never to lose my self again.

In Calgary, I had never felt alone - even when I first moved into my condominium and had not met my soon-to-become friends. I felt safe and secure in my condominium community, although I had really missed Manitoba sunsets and the hot summer nights of the prairies. There is nothing like Manitoba anywhere. They rival a sunset over the ocean on a tropical island.

Now I was back in a house, in suburban Winnipeg. It was a four-bedroom, two-story house. There was only me, my dog and my bird. What was I doing in such a big place?

Well, because I had gotten it at such an excellent price, I could not pass it up. I figured that I would hold onto it as an investment. Then, if I kept it for five to seven years, I would sell and be able to afford to retire early.

In the meantime, I would have lots of room for my grandson and my friends to visit and I would be able to convert one bedroom into a home office, as I was to work from home for the next 4-6 months, while changes were taking place at the Winnipeg work office.

By now, it had been almost three years since I had left John and a marriage that had lasted 28 years. I look back at all those cold, lonely, empty years, and think "What a waste!" Almost three years had gone by since I left John…since we had had a fight over a $5. Plant and since I had gone for that long walk and decided that our marriage was over; that there was absolutely nothing left - no love, no hate - nothing.

I understand how hurt John must have felt. He had ignored all the warnings for years and never believed I would leave. I guess he had thought that he did not need to put any effort into our marriage and that I would continue to take whatever he dished out. Somehow, this time, I had decided to leave. I had not known how or when, but I knew it was going to happen and I was the only one who could make it happen.

I look back at how unhappy and uncertain I had been and I look at where I am now. I am amazed at what I have accomplished and how far I have grown, in so short a time. The experiences I have gone through since leaving John…some have been painful, some have been joyful, but all have helped me move forward.

When I think back to that scared and hurt person who felt like she was in a prison with no idea how to get out, I cannot believe the changes that have happened in my life since. It was a very painful time, but I have evolved into a much stronger, confident person. Most important, I am now my own person. I do not have to compromise who I am - my "self" - for anyone else.

I do not have to worry about or take care of anyone else but me, for the first time since I have been 19 years old. It has felt funny and lonely at times but it is getting easier, and I do not fight being alone anymore. I made a promise to myself that instead of evolving through pain, I resolve to evolve through Joy and Happiness from now one.

In my quest to find a spiritual community, I came across some fascinating information:

Because Winnipeg lies at the heart centre of the North American continent, it is a powerful spiritual energy vortex center akin to Cathedral Grove, British Columbia or Sedona, Arizona.

Kelly McKennon from Palouse, Idaho, USA has developed a special gift for sensing qui, which is, in his understanding, the Chinese word for energy, quite accurately. A few years ago, he started a systematic quest for revitalizing energy vortices that had been compromised with negative energy. He observed that freeing these vortices was leading to the build-up of a continuous canopy of positive life energy.

His quest has led him around the globe and he has written an ongoing account of his work on the ethericwarriors.com forum under the title "Heaven and Earth."

On the return journey, due to a missed connection, he had a flight from Amsterdam direct to Seattle, which passed over northeastern Canada. About the middle of Hudson's Bay, as the route of the plane turned south over the province of Manitoba to his surprise, he observed the edge of an energy canopy directly over Winnipeg.

There is a special place in Winnipeg called "The Sanctuary," a place for prayer, meditation, and healing. It has a sacred vortex or energy, which enhances spiritual work. This special place is known as The Christic Heart of North America. The Sanctuary facilitates the connection with Higher-Self as well as individual and global healing. In an atmosphere of loving acceptance of all, regardless of denomination, The Sanctuary offers opportunities for personal growth, healing and spiritual illumination.

An Awakening

I have been born anew.
Like Venus from the shell
I awoke full and whole.
Ready to face the world as I am.

Facets of my soul
Long dormant have found voice.
You have released me from my slumber.
With you I am made whole.
Through you I am free.

Steps on the path
Now before me.
Confident I am making
The right choices.
Knowing you are with me,
Loving, caring, trusting.
Brave new world
Here I am.
A soul found.

Raymond A. Foss

CHAPTER 17

Finding My Life Purpose

August 1998

Time passed so swiftly. Three months had just flown by, and Suzanne was moving back to Winnipeg. She lived with me for a few months, while looking for a condo. She found the perfect condominium only five minutes away from mine. She had some renovations done while she stayed with me and we had a wonderful time being together again. It was bizarre how we both were from Winnipeg, both moved to Calgary in order to meet, and then both moved back to Winnipeg, through our jobs.

That fall, I got a serious bout of pneumonia, and Suzanne suggested that I go see her girlfriend Linda Foreman. Linda had been a nurse at St. Boniface Hospital for over 30 years and she had since left that to become a Reiki Master. This was the first I had heard of Reiki and did not quite know what to expect, but made an appointment for a Reiki healing session.

Since I had never heard about Reiki before, I looked it up, and read the following: Reiki is a natural healing art. Reiki allows anyone to channel the ever-present Universal Life Energy promoting healing of mind, body, and spirit. Reiki is deep relaxation therapy, done through the laying of hands on the person, to comfort and relieve pain. This is done in connection with the Universal energy in conjunction with your own energy, through the Reiki practitioner.

I was amazed at the results of that Reiki session, and that I knew this was what I was meant to do. I could see myself doing it and loving it.

I found Reiki - or did Reiki find me? That was a life-changing event for me. Before I left there, I asked Linda, "What does Reiki mean?"

She explained: "Reiki (Ray-key) means Universal Life Energy in Japanese. It is a simple, powerful, and effective natural art of channeling healing energy through the hands. Dr. Mikao Usui rediscovered this healing art in Japan in the early eighteenth century. Reiki promotes healing of physical, emotional, and spiritual imbalances. Reiki greatly enhances the healer's vitality and even protects the healer from taking another's condition."

I asked her how I could learn to do Reiki and signed up

 immediately for Reiki, Level 1. That same week, I took my Reiki, Level 1 on November 30, 1998 and received my Reiki, Level I Certificate, along with three other students.

Learning Reiki involves attending a class where you go through an opening process (called an attunement), which activates and increases your ability to channel Universal Life Force. Class includes instructions on how to give a Reiki treatment for general maintenance and for specific conditions, as well as the history of Reiki and discussions of its uses. The desire to learn and the opening process is all you need to begin healing with Reiki.

I immediately started to do Reiki on myself and on others. I discovered that Reiki calms the mind, nourishes the body and the spirit with the gentle yet powerful energy. It is so easy and can be learned by everyone. A Reiki attunement will connect you with the Universal Life Force Energy, enabling you to give Reiki treatments to yourself and to others.

The more I did Reiki sessions on myself and/or others, the more intuitive and attuned I became to the needs of the different clients. The first few months, I worked mainly on family members, pets, my plants, and myself. I used it for greater health and well-being, as well as for pain relief, profound relaxation, and acceleration of the body's normal healing process.

What does Reiki do?

Reiki is suitable for both healthy and sick people of all ages. It is a divine bond between the healer and the healee. The physical contact conveys love, warmth and a sense of satisfaction at the mental level. Reiki also creates confidence, in both the healer and the client.

Reiki relaxes the mind, and helps deal with the cause of various diseases at the physical, mental, psychological, and deeper spiritual levels. Strain is physical, stress and depression are mental or psychological, - all of which can be treated effectively by Reiki.

Through the use of Reiki healing energy, one can heal headaches, body tension, migraines, backaches, exhaustion, overweight, hormonal changes and imbalances, colds, allergies, influenza, digestive and other stomach disorders, gall and kidney stones, ulcers, inflammations, arthritis, cancer and other chronic diseases.

Reiki is very helpful in eliminating fears and phobias hidden in the subconscious through the techniques of "mental healing." Reiki promotes "Self-healing." Reiki treatments for oneself, early in the morning or last thing at night, enhances ones own energy level.

Reiki can also be applied directly as "First Aid" as it helps to stop bleeding and speeds up the healing process. Reiki is a tool for use at any moment, any time, anywhere, for on-the-spot stress release, pain relief, and quick energy.

Reiki is safe and can be combined with any other medical therapies, such as Homeopathy, Acupuncture, Reflexology, and others. Reiki is a complementary alternative healing method. For proper diagnosis, always consult a physician. Never discontinue medicine or medical advice without consulting your own doctor.

Reiki is simply about energy and it is a system in which to apply this energy into your daily life. Reiki is not a religion and holds no doctrines, creeds, or contradictions to the Universal Laws of Consciousness and Love. It is one of the few forms of healing that can be used to heal self.

To recap: Reiki is a holistic self-help technique for directing natural life energy. No special environment or equipment is needed and age makes no difference. By following easy to learn steps, anyone is able to direct the "light energy" of Reiki to meet their own individual needs.

Healing Benefits of Reiki

Strengthens Immune System
Relaxes mind, body and soul
Removes fears and phobias

Heals aches and pains
Heals healer also
Heals at all levels

Aids sleep and digestion
Eases suffering
Promotes spiritual growth

Enhances healing powers
Reduces stress and anxiety
Provides distance healing

Removes toxic substances
Boosts energy and stamina
Balances energy

Purifies and revitalizes chakras
Relieves symptoms of diseases
In Reiki, Level 1, you will learn:

What is Reiki?
History of Reiki
How to Practice Reiki
Healing Others
How to Start Reiki Flowing
Other Uses for Reiki
Affirmations

Tips on Choosing a Reiki Master as a Teacher

People choose a Reiki teacher in many different ways. Sometimes, life unfolds in synchronistic order. You meet someone and feel attracted to his or her style and energy, then find out they happen to be a Reiki Master. On the other hand, while doing a search, a particular name, photo, or address resonates with you and you feel you are meant to learn with that person. Alternatively, you book a session with a Reiki Master, on the recommendation of a friend and connect immediately with that person, (this is what happened to me).

At other times, no obvious "signs" or "signals" present themselves. You may wish to phone around to a few different teachers and ask questions about things such as their training and teaching philosophies. Reiki involves no religion, dogma, or system of belief, and requires no special state of being. Anyone of any age, occupation, or lifestyle can become a Reiki Healer.

If you are considering learning Reiki for the first time, or wish to take a new level of training. I would be pleased to chat with you and answer any questions you may have such as: work background,

Reiki training, teaching styles and philosophy, role as Reiki Master, understanding of Reiki, schedule, fees and what you receive in exchange…how they get the caramel in the Caramel bar…or anything else you are pondering. Check out my website: for further information. Most importantly, do your own research and listen to your instincts. You will know, just as I knew.

Now that I had this knowledge under my belt, I realized this was what all the psychics and mediums had been seeing for me all these years. They all said I was a healer, and would work in that field. I could not see me as a nurse or health-care worker, but I could see me as a Reiki practitioner…yes!

The first client that I had: Client A had recently had chemotherapy for throat cancer, and they had told him he probably would not be able to talk again, as it was highly probable that his vocal cords were permanently damaged.

As we did the Reiki healing, I could feel my hands vibrating over his throat area, becoming almost uncomfortably hot. However, whenever I thought of moving my hands away, I found them to be almost frozen over the area, and unwilling to move. Trusting the guidance, I left my hands over his throat area for quite a long time – perhaps twenty to thirty minutes. Finally, my hands unlocked and I was able to move on to complete the entire body healing.

After the session ended, he said to me that he could feel the heat of my hands and then he could feel a big black cloud rising from the chest and throat and moving around in a vortex around the throat area. It kept getting faster and faster, until it disintegrated into a big puff of smoke and was gone. He felt like he could breathe again. Over the next month, his voice became stronger and stronger and he regained the full use of his vocal cords. That was a "wow" moment for both of us.

Client B who came to me for a Reiki Session had had a heart defect from birth. He was 42 years old, very pale, and ill. He was on the waiting list for heart replacement surgery, which was to take place in Toronto, at a moment's notice. He was very anxious about this and wanted to keep his energy up to survive the grueling surgery and post-operative healing.

While doing the Reiki healing session, I had a vision of a past-life for him where he was a Native American Indian. He was sitting down in front of his teepee, children playing around the fire in front of him. He was stripping the meat off a buffalo, giving it over to the women, who were laying it out on a string over the fire, to smoke and cure it. Suddenly, five warriors on horses attacked them and before he had a chance to take up arms to defend himself and his family, he received a long spear directly to the heart, dying instantly.

After the session, I told him of this vision and then we prayed together to release the cell memory associated with that trauma…that this was a different lifetime and to give it up to God and allow the white light to come into his heart. He said that he felt so much more energetic after that session.

He continued coming for sessions once or twice a month,

whenever his energy force became very low, for over two years. One day he received the call that there was a heart waiting for him. He flew to Toronto, had the heart transplant, it all went well. He came back home and has resumed a normal, healthy life, to this day.

Client C: was a northern Manitoban aboriginal woman. During the Reiki session, I saw a white owl, a chair, a boat, a cougar, and seagulls. My interpretation was that the white owl was her spirit guide and to call on him often for help. Guides never interfere; you must ask for their help, assistance, love, and protection. The chair indicated she needed a period of rest and recuperation. She needed to take time out, to be open to other opportunities. The boat indicated her need to consider how to handle isolation and the ability to be alone. It also represented how she coped with her own emotions and those of others and how to navigate her way through life, for control of life. The cougar represented her link to her feline, sensuous side: to be aware of the two sides to her nature, one devious and one helpful. It also indicated her powerful, self-sufficient aspects. Seagulls are a symbol of freedom and power.

She told me that she had been asking for the name of her spirit guide and seeing white owls everywhere in the past few months, in the woods, in her dreams, and so I was confirming what she instinctively knew all along…that indeed, "White Owl" was the name of her spirit guide.

SEARCHING

My ship sails out unto the ocean of wide open spaces
It's hull creaking with the souls of all the people's faces
A destiny of unknown dreams and desires,
Burning within me, the coals from fires

I can not see the dreams of unknown shores
My body is weakened by life's tasking chores
Still I search onward to find a peaceful meaning
Like a giant tree, aged and leaning

What will I find and what will it all mean to me
I look into my mirror and my reflection I can see
Can I be happy and can I have my love
Graceful and beautiful as the morning dove

Like the wind that puts life into my sails
Like the skies of blue and winding trails
Oh, Lord show me the way and hold onto me tight
Oh, Lord show me the way and show me the light.

Rick Thompson

CHAPTER 18

Meditation and Manifesting Your Destiny

September 1998

S uzanne and I took a private meditation class and I started meditating every morning, consistently, and writing down in a journal whatever was coming through.

I also took the Nightingale-Conant 12-hour course on Manifesting Your Destiny, by Dr. Wayne Dyer. He says, "Within you is a divine capacity to manifest and attract all that you need or desire."

"Can you imagine being able to manifest anything you want in life? You can make problems go away by themselves and bring every joy and reward your heart truly desires into your life. Think about it. You have already seen the results in your own life.

You accomplish those things that you truly believe you are capable of doing: what you focus on and have no doubts about really does come to pass; your life is shaped by the things you spend the most time thinking about."

Dr. Dyer's program teaches how to:

- Trust in your higher self and in the wisdom of creation
- Understand that what you desire also desires you
- Realize that solutions to problems lie within
- Accept that you are one with the world around you
- Feel worthy to receive your desires
- Achieve a perfect state of awareness through meditation
- Acknowledge your oneness with the universal energy that manifests your desires.

The capacity to manifest is more than a power within you. It is the power of life itself. In addition, in this transformational program, Dr. Dyer teaches you how to overcome your conditioning and grant yourself the power to know that manifesting your desires is possible. You can have everything you want in life once you learn the secrets to manifesting your destiny.

I highly recommend it to all. I will never regret the excellent investment of time and money. You have to know what you want and make sure that is what you really, really want. Then, write it down so that when you get it, you remember that you asked for it. The third thing is, Ask!

Imagine your fairy godmother is standing before you, ready to wave her wand and make your wishes come true. Suddenly, the world appears a different place, full of possibilities and magic! Well, it turns out that this imaginary scenario is actually how the process of manifestation works—and is based, not in magic, but in science. Science vividly explains this powerful universal principle called the Law of Attraction, which simply stated is, like attracts like.

Whatever we think, feel and put our energy into, whether positive or negative, we magnetize to us. The universe, like a good fairy godmother, simply responds. That sounds easy enough, right.

So, why don't we all have everything we want? The answer lies in my favorite formula for applying the Law of Attraction. It has three simple, easy-to-remember steps:

1. INTENTION – Be clear about what you want
2. ATTENTION – Experience the thoughts and feelings of already having what you want, AND take the action steps to manifest your intention.
3. NO TENSION – Let go. Relax. Shift from being tightly focused on your specific desired outcome to being wide open to all possibilities. Trust that your highest good will come to you, and feel the happiness of that.

A lot has been written and spoken about the first two steps. Many of us have mastered them, but have stopped there. We end up holding on to our desire like a terrier chewing on a bone. We have to take action towards our goals, but when we push, struggle, and hold on too tight, we get in our own way. It is like writing a letter, bringing it to the mailbox, and hanging onto it, instead of letting it go and trusting it will reach its destination, without having to guide it every step of the way.

Let it go. Tell yourself "no regrets." The past is finished. You do not change the outcome by going over it. I used to think that the 28 years that I had been married were wasted years. However, I understand now that whatever the past gave us in experiences, it was something we had to know, or do. I am a better person now because of what I went through all those years. I had to go there to get here. I understand and accept it and that has enabled me to move on.

The problem is when we have not taken the last step. We have not let go. We have not surrendered. We have not said, "Okay, this or something better." The third step, "no tension," frees our minds, opens our heart, and, most importantly, lets us be happy in this moment.

If we skip this step, it is like having a closed fist; how can we receive anything when our hand isn't open? In our "gotta-get" culture, this is the step most people miss or dismiss. When we let go and trust that all is ultimately working out for the best, we feel happier. In addition, happiness attracts more happiness.

When I first heard about this formula, I had an "ah-ha moment." I realized that every time I had succeeded in manifesting my desires, it had happened only after I had done step #3, let go, relaxed, and felt happy. In fact, here is a perfect example of this.

By now, in 1998, I had been working for eighteen years as a corporate trainer and senior account manager. I had been Regional Manager, the top echelon for women in my company, for my area. To move upwards, I would have to move far away from family and friends. I was burnt out from a divorce three years before. I was still trying to figure out who I really was, and where to go from here.

I had been told that I was a "healer" from many psychics throughout my life but could not see myself in the mainstream healing industry. I had recently been introduced to Reiki, had taken the first level, and felt that this could be what I was looking for, to retire from corporate life, and do to something more meaningful.

I was told, through a medium, that "spirit" wanted me to plan, yes...but then to trust, not visualize every single aspect of my life, which was very difficult for me (type A personality) to do.

My intention was clear (step #1): to inspire and empower people to live their lives to their highest and best potential, by learning how to heal themselves and others, through Reiki and other healing therapies. My attention was focused on thinking, feeling, and visualizing success, by starting my own Company and being able to work from home. (Step #2).

Needing to take a break, I decided to go to the mountains by myself for two weeks to meditate on my life. After a few days of silence—no easy feat for me—the most amazing thing happened. I began to tap into something deeper in myself, and started to feel peaceful, relaxed, and fulfilled. I moved into that state of no tension, where my grip on achieving my goal melted away, leaving me with a feeling of deep contentment.

Then, on the fourth day of silence, while I was sitting quietly in meditation, a light bulb went off in my head, and I clearly saw the words: Healing Harmony of Life being a circle where the healing of the body, mind, and spirit/soul is done in harmony with each other, rather than in isolation of one another.

This was in 1998, when not much was out there about treating the person in this way. Established medicine was still ignoring the value of other healing therapies, such as vitamins, homeopathy, aromatherapy, hydrotherapy, healing through sound, light, among others.

The minute I got home, I registered my new Company, "Healing Trilogy," opened a business bank account, understanding that the Universe hates a vacuum and will rush to fill it. Then, I started preparing a "healing room" in my house, emptied a bedroom, set up the closet as a desk for healing supplies, a sound system, and a waterfall therapy system.

In January, I asked the Universe...if I am meant to do Reiki and work with Reiki, then, I need a massage therapy table. As I figured out my finances, I could only afford three hundred dollars. Therefore, as a test, I asked God...if you want me to do this work...if this is what I am meant to do in this lifetime, then show me in this way...send me a massage therapy table for $300.

In the meantime, I looked in the papers occasionally, in the buy-sell, phoned the massage therapy department, looked at new massage therapy tables...none were in the price range that I could afford. I was not frantic in my search. I trusted that at the right time, this would come my way.

Then, I developed my Company Logo, registered my company name with the Provincial Government of Manitoba "Business Names Registration Office." This is my logo, letterhead, and business card.

Logo

Healing Trilogy
For the Mind, Body, and Soul

Reiki Healing, Light Massage Therapy, Cranio-Sacral Therapy,
Chakra Clearing, Meditation Sessions, Other Healing Workshops & Seminars

Estelle Reder
Reiki Master

199 Eastmount Drive, MB R2N 3W9
Tel: (204) 257-2142 email: estelle104@hotmail.com
Website: www.healingtrilogy.com

Business Card

199 Eastmount Drive, Winnipeg, MB. Canada R2N 3W9
Email: Estelle.reder@gmail.com Website: www.healingtrilogy.com
Phone/fax: (204) 257-2142

Letterhead

I also registered with the Holistic Practitioners' Network. For a reliable list of practitioners, to register or to see who works in that field, go to www.holisticpractitionersnetwork.com

WE WILL RECEIVE POWER

We are waiting as they were
ready, waiting, trusting, living in community
for the fulfillment of this promise
that we will receive power, that we
will be given what we need, by the holy spirit
equipping us, to spread Christ's love
God's love to the ends of the earth
that we will be infused, emboldened, enabled
at God's appointed time, a divine appointment
to spread the message of love
to the outermost reaches, the whole world

Raymond A. Foss

CHAPTER 19

You Don't Ask, You Don't Get

May 1999

I got a phone call from my friend Maureen, in Calgary. We chatted a while. She asked what I was working on, so I casually mentioned that I was still looking for a massage therapy table, to set up my business when I retired (which was still a few years away). I was only 52 years old at the time. I did not mention price or anything else to Maureen.

She immediately told me she had been at her massage therapist the night before and he was shutting down his business, due to carpal tunnel. She said, "I'll call him, and I'll call you right back." and quickly hung up.

She called me back within fifteen minutes and said, "He'll give you his entire supply of towels, his aromatherapy oils, his special pillows, his fitted sheets and his massage table - all for... (you guessed it)... $300."

Wow, that blew me away. Not only did the Universe deliver...it delivered more than I ever expected. I drove out to pick it up.

I came home after staying with Maureen, catching up with old friends and daily driving to the mountains to meditate. I had my massage therapy table, which I set up and slowly started to give private Reiki sessions.

I am certain that it was by using all three steps of this powerful formula—intention, attention, and no tension—that I was able to realize my dream. Any two of the steps would not have done it.

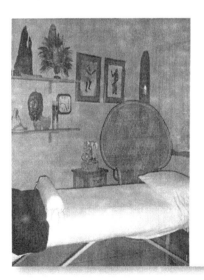

So, did I live happily ever after? Not right away. After using this formula for many years to attract extraordinary situations, people, and things that I wanted, I eventually realized, like many people before me, that having the things and circumstances you want in your life is wonderful AND it is not enough. It was then that I discovered another essential key: there is more.

Having things and circumstances – money, success, relation-ships, health—brings a certain happiness, what I call being "happy for good reason." Unfortunately, this temporary experience of satisfaction or joy soon fades and we have to hurry up and fulfill the next desire to get a new high.

To experience true and lasting happiness, we must be free of the need for any external reason to be happy. As Deepak Chopra has said, "happiness for a reason is just another form of misery."

What we all want most deeply is to be what I have come to call "happy for no reason"—a lasting neurophysiologic state of peace and well-being that is not dependent on circumstances. The good news is this is an achievable state.

Ironically, we seem to have things backwards. True happiness is not a result of getting what we want; getting what we want is a side effect of happiness. Why? Because, when we are happy for no reason, we have mastered that tricky step #3, no tension, and then our desires manifest more quickly and effortlessly than ever.

Perhaps we need to focus a little less on getting what we want to make us happy and a little more on creating a deep inner state of happiness. When we are happy for no reason, all else is just icing on the cake. That is the ultimate secret!

Depend on God to make you happy and allow the universe to meet your needs. When a need arises, trust that you will receive exactly what you need. Write it down, so that when you get it, you will remember you asked for it.

If you do not get it, well, the universe has a different plan for you. Most of the time, you do not need half of what you think you do. If you go back six months later and check what you wrote down that you wanted, you will see that the things you did not get, you did not need to get you where you are in this moment. It works every time!

Once you have a breakthrough, it is like a water shed. It just comes at you from all sides at once. When you begin to live consciously, to monitor your thoughts throughout to day, you realize that you attract more of whatever you're thinking. I realized that for me, things came at me in three's.

Then, I read about the power of three. Do you want to know how to create your world the way you want and desire it to be? Ask and it is given. "You don't ask…you don't get." Do not be afraid to ask the Universe for what you want. Ask often. The Universe is abundant. There is enough for everyone.

Start with this prayer or intention: "Father God, Mother Azna (or Universal Energy).My Guardian Angel and all my Spirit Guides. This day and always, I ask for your guidance, assistance, love, and protection…For the good and benefit of all."

Be careful what you ask for…You might get it. As an example: This man asked to win the lottery, and won $16 Million. His only brother tried to have him killed and he is now serving a life sentence. He invested in a restaurant, lost everything; his health deteriorated, and he is poorer now than prior to winning...that's why you need to add at the end of each and every request: "For the good and benefit of all."

Ask the Godhead[f] for three things. Be very specific...give details -.shape, color, size. Think about what you do, why you do it. What do you really, really want to do, and why do you want to do it? Talk and share this with people who you trust will support you in a positive way.

Write it down, so that when you get it you will remember what you asked for. Start writing in a journal; communicate with yourself... stories, anecdotes, your dreams... what you really, really want. Write it out. Think about the human aspect of what you do, how what you do at work affects people in a positive way.

Things happen in three's...pay attention. It is no coincidence, as there is no such thing as a coincidence. Examples: The Trinity, The Three Wise Men, knock three times, three blind mice (just kidding on that one!). However, things do happen for a reason. The universe is guiding you towards a certain path, person, or thing.

So, in the morning, light a white candle; ask the Universe for three things today, be very specific... It is okay to ask for money. However, the universe does not understand money, dollars, and cents. You ask instead for the abundance of financial energy. The universe understands abundance, energy, and financial matters.

---

[f] Godhead = Father God, Mother Azna, or Universal Energy...whatever you are comfortable with, it doesn't matter what you call it, it is the intent that counts.

You Don't Ask, You Don't Get   181

Test three places when you want to ask for something. Be careful what you ask for…you might get it! To make sure you are asking for the right things; check if it feels right mentally (in your head). What is your brain thinking? Check in your heart. What is it feeling? Check with the stomach. What does your gut tell you?

If those three are okay, proceed with your request. If one of them is telling you no, stop and think it out before going ahead.

After you have asked for three things, always finish your request with "for the good and benefit of one and all." If your request fulfilled would wind up hurting someone or changing you to become greedy or mean, then, you don't want it, right? "What matters if you've conquered the world, if you've lost your soul in the attempt?"

This lifetime will go by quickly; your soul will go on infinitely. Think about it. By living consciously, being in the moment, in the "now," you will start recognizing opportunities that are presented to you.

When an idea or the thought of someone comes to your mind once, pay attention. Twice, take notice. Three times…do something about it. The universe is sending you a message, take action!

As an example of this - I now had my massage therapy table, my company, a few clients, and I was teaching Reiki. Things were going great. Then, one day, I asked the Universe if there was something else that I needed to learn to incorporate into the Reiki Healing Sessions.

Later that same day, I turned on the television and there is a program about "CranioSacral Therapy." I had never heard about it before, so sat there enthralled about this technique. The next day, I received my monthly Chatelaine magazine, and there is a two-page cover story on "CranioSacral Therapy."

An osteopath, Dr. William Sutherland, developed CranioSacral Therapy in the early nineteenth century. Massage and physical therapists, chiropractors and naturopathic doctors, as well as alternative healing practitioners use it.

CranioSacral Therapy is a gentle, hands-on form of body therapy that evaluates and enhances a physiological system called the cranioSacral system. It is comprised of the membranes and cerebrospinal fluid that surrounds and protects the brain and spinal cord. Using a soft touch, often no heavier than the weight of a nickel, practitioners can release restrictions in the CranioSacral system to improve the functioning of the central nervous system.

Then, I called my girlfriend Melody Jones in Regina, just to chat and she told me she just took a course that weekend on (you guessed it)...CranioSacral Therapy.

There it was...three times...pay attention, right. Before I started living consciously, I would not have made the connection, but now that I was paying attention, it was coming to me from all sides.

First, I phoned Toronto and found they would charge me $1400. for this course plus airfare and accommodation for two days. Yikes, I could not afford that!

Secondly, I checked around Winnipeg. There was no one who was offering this course locally.

My third attempt was to phone Melody to get more information. Her contact was a nun, Sister Florence Leduc, who was 82 years old, blind, and still teaching all these courses. An amazing woman! Melody did not think she would be running this course in the near future. However, I called her directly, remembering, "You don't ask, you don't get."

In our phone conversation, I explained my situation. After a short pause, she said, "Why don't you drive out on the upcoming long weekend and stay with Melody on Sunday. Then, come to

see me Monday morning and I'll do the course for you for one hundred dollars - incorporating all the teachings into one day. Wow! It still gives me goose bumps when I think about how the Universe worked to give me this course.

It was awesome. This woman was an angel on earth. Sister Leduc had a B.A. and B.Ed. She was a Professor in Hypnotherapy, a Reiki Master/Teacher, a CranioSacral Therapist, and a Body Reading Practitioner and worked with clients in behavior modification, pain control and stress management.

While she was teaching me one of the Cranio-sacral positions to use while doing a Reiki session, she casually mentioned to me..."Do you know your guardian angel?"

I replied, "Yes, Melody introduced him to me a few years ago."

She continued: "But, have you ever seen him yourself?"

I answered: "No, I've never been able to see him, yet."

Then, she said, "Well, I see him, right now...he is so close to you, and he guards you so fiercely. He is a tall warrior and he actually resides in your aura...that's how closely he guards you."

Well, that blew me away!

Remember, Melody had introduced me to my guardian angel, while living in Calgary. She said his name was "Fieronan...the fierce warrior." I had not talked about my guardian angel to anyone, so when she told me this, it completely bowled me over. She also taught me how to do "Body Reading," a sort-of "muscle testing." That was a bonus, thrown in that day!

In the Body Reading section, Sister Leduc taught me how to read and trust myself. She explained that when you are faced with a decision, for example, buying one kind of vitamin versus another kind. Hold the object in the hands, and ask yourself, "Is this vitamin what my body needs right now?" Close your eyes, and if your body sways forward, this is a "yes" answer, and if your body sways backwards, this is a "no" answer. Too easy? Yes, it is that easy!

PART V

Endings and Beginnings

(2001)

WINGS OF THE ANGELS

A gentle wind blew cross the land
Reaching out to take a hand
For on the winds the angels came
Calling out a father's name.

Left behind, the children's tears
Loving memories of the years
Of joy and love, a life well spent
And now to God a father's sent.

On angel's wings, a heavenly flight
The journey home, towards the light
To those who weep, a life is gone
But in God's love, 'tis but the dawn.

Tim Chambers

CHAPTER 20

Dad's Journey Home

March 2001

I decided to find a Reiki Master for Level II (as my Level I teacher, Linda Foreman, had moved to Ontario to help her aging parents). Karen Deley, who had taught Suzanne, Karen Lefebvre and me meditation techniques, suggested Cheryl Whitebone and we were not disappointed.

Karen Lefebvre and I immediately signed up for the class. Cheryl Whitebone, Reiki Master and Teacher, guided us through the class. Second Degree Reiki consists of a set of three Sanskrit Symbols, with a designated energy for each symbol that increases the effectiveness of the channeled Reiki energy.

The three symbols are used during a regular hands-on Reiki treatment to increase the power of the channeled energy. They are also used to direct the Reiki energy through time and space. The Distance Symbol can also be used to bridge time; you can use it to send Reiki into the future or into the past. If you or someone you know will be involved in an important activity in the future, you can send Reiki to the date and time of the event so that it will be there to help you.

If you or someone you know had a traumatic experience in the past, you can use the Distance Symbol to send Reiki back to heal the trauma. The Reiki will not change the event, but it will change how you see, feel, and understand the experience. This may make it possible to change the impact that the trauma has had upon your life. This technique can also be used to deal with situations that arise from past lives.

Reiki can be sent over long distances - across the room, across the world or across time. The process of sending Reiki across the room to a client who is physically present is called beaming. One must always ask permission before sending Reiki energy to anyone, present or absent. It is possible to ask permission on the soul level if you are unable to speak directly to the person. This capability is excellent for sending healing energy to anyone undergoing surgery, long stays at hospitals, etc.

After completing my Reiki, Level II, when visiting my dad in the nursing home, I asked him if I could do healing on him. I explained to him what Reiki was and he said, "Well, it can't hurt, so go for it." He loved it so much and felt better for days after I had done Reiki on him. After that, every time I went to visit, he would immediately go lie down on his bed and say: "Do that healing thing on me."

When I could not go for a visit, I would send him long-distance Reiki, after my morning meditation. It was a great comfort to both of us. Earlier that year, the entire family, with dad, had met with the doctor and nurses at the nursing home. They asked us what we wanted to do, should something happen to dad. We all turned to him and said, "Dad, what do you want?"

He looked at all of us with such love in his eyes and tearfully replied, "I want to go home to be with your mom. Let me go. Do not prolong my life in any way. Just keep me comfortable until I go." We all had tears in our eyes, as we promised him it would be as he asked.

September 2001

In early September, dad had a stroke. A few days later, he had a second stroke. I went to see him and he looked so frail and feeble. I was scheduled to go on a business trip to Burlington, Ontario the next day. I asked the doctor if he thought I should go or if I should stay close to home. "No," he replied, "You go to your business meetings. Your dad is quite stable now and he should be okay for the next week.

I said good-bye with foreboding in my heart. I felt helpless, but what could I do? I left for my business trip. I had just settled into my hotel room, in Hamilton, Ontario when I got a call from home that dad had had a third stroke and that I should come home immediately.

I quickly packed, advised my boss that I had been called home on an urgent family matter, and returned. We had called ahead, and because it was a family emergency, the airline had found me a seat on the next flight out. Someone had given up a seat for me. I was incredibly thankful to that "unknown angel."

Four hours later, I was back home, changed, and drove out to the nursing home. They had moved him from his small room into a special family room, where we could have privacy. Someone had even donated a pullout sofa for people to lie down, during the waiting.

The waiting - waiting for someone to pass over to the other side - this is very painful for everyone...for the one going into the unknown and for the ones left behind, bereft.

Dad and I had talked often about death and dying. He was not scared. He had been seeing Mom in his room almost every day for the past month or so, and so he knew the end was near.

I told him: "Dad...the other side is only one step up to get over...it's not up there in the sky." That's all you need to do...Mom will be there, among others, to welcome you home."

The nurse came often to check on him, and she would give us reports on his vital statistics. By around 6:00 p.m. that night, she said that his lungs were starting to fill up and that he would be getting very distressed and be in pain. She said for us to say our good-byes, as the morphine would put him out and he would not be able to talk or recognize us from that time on.

All eleven of us were there, surrounding his bed and we each gave him a hug, told him how much we loved him and thanked him for the great life he had given us. I was holding on to his hand, doing continual Reiki on him when I told him "Dad, its okay to go, now. Do you want us to sing to you, while the nurse gives you the medicine that will take you home to the other side?"

With the last smile that he could muster, he said, "Yes, I would love that." Dad had always been very proud of us as a musical family. Everyone in the family knew how to play at least one instrument, and most family gatherings were around the piano, with guitars, violins, flute, drums, and whatever new instrument someone was experimenting with at the time.

Therefore, I asked all the siblings to join me in singing until dad was no longer conscious. We sang, both in French and in English:

> *"Into Your Hands, We Commend His Spirit, O Lord.*
> *Into Your Hands, We Commend His Life.*
> *For it's in dying, that we are born again.*
> *Into Your Hands, We Commend our Dad."*

Dad passed over to spirit September 11, 2001. Yes, the same day that the terrorists flew two planes into the Twin Towers in New York City that sent thousands to the other side all at once. He was released from his body at 6:00 a.m. on September 12, 2001

TOUCHED BY AN ANGEL

We, unaccustomed to courage
exiles from delight
live coiled in shells of loneliness
until love leaves its high holy temple
and comes into our sight
to liberate us into life

Love arrives
and in its train come ecstasies
old memories of pleasure
ancient histories of pain.
Yet if we are bold,
love strikes away the chains of fear
from our souls.

We are weaned from our timidity
In the flush of love's light
we dare be brave
And suddenly we see
that love costs all we are
and will ever be.
Yet it is only love
which sets us free.

Maya Angelou

194   That's My Story

CHAPTER 21

Healing Practice and
Spiritual Growth

September 2001

Earlier that year, my girlfriend from Calgary, Maureen, had met a man through Match.com. They had co-rresponded for over three months before even meeting each other. They liked each other on site and dated the rest of that year, culminating in their getting married in the Cook Islands over Christmas. I was so happy for them.

I would go out to visit once or twice a year and Maureen would come out to Winnipeg as well. She kept prodding me to join Match.com. For some reason, I was resisting.

In the meantime, I had asked my angel guides to

send me a Reiki Master to take the Usui Reiki Master/Teacher Level. My teacher for Reiki Level II, Cheryl Whitebone, had moved out to Nova Scotia, on the East coast of Canada, but it turned out that they were being transferred to Edmonton, Alberta, in Western Canada, and that she would be able to spend a few weeks in Winnipeg during the move. She agreed to teach seven of us who wanted to become Reiki Masters/Teachers. (Isn't it amazing how the Universe conspires to bring you what you need, exactly when you need it?)

Over an intensive weekend starting Friday night, all day Saturday, and all day Sunday, we took the training that included:

- Discussion on the meaning of mastery
- Attunement to the Usui Master Symbol
- Reiki Meditations
- Reiki breath and Reiki movement exercises
- Two Tibetan Reiki symbols
- Creating and Using a Reiki Centre
- Channeling Reiki
- Instructions and practice in giving all attunements
- Information on how to structure Reiki classes
- Information on how to develop your Reiki practice.

We were to ask a question, which would be answered by spirit during the Reiki Meditation. My question was, "Is Dad okay on the other side?" It was an overcast, cloudy afternoon, but at that moment that I formulated my question, the sun came through the living room window, shining its full beam directly on me. I had my answer. Dad had made it home and he was happy.

Part of the training included meditating and receiving a master symbol, which is different for each person. This symbol is used in the attunement process. It clears the energy of the recipient, and prepares her to receive the Reiki energy and symbols. The Master Symbol acts as an anchor for the Reiki energy in the human energy system.

The five symbols to choose from were:

Christianity   Judaism   Buddhism

Islam   Hinduism

I just loved all the symbols except the Christianity one. I guess that being brought up a Catholic; I had always felt guilty for "causing" Jesus' death, in atonement for our sins, as the teachings went. To my way of thinking, Jesus was not my hero or someone I could admire. After all, he got himself hung like a common criminal. Therefore, I was concentrating on all the other symbols, except the cross. When we did our meditation, of course, that which you resists comes to you…my symbol was definitely the cross…I even saw it in 3-D. Therefore, I accepted Jesus as my master symbol.

After that, I decided to read up on the life of Jesus, that there had to be more to it than his sacrificing his life for us on the cross. That's when I came across the Ascended Masters and learned that Jesus wasn't the only one…there are many others: Buddha (Asia), Isis (Egypt), Krishna (Hindu-India), Kuan Yin (Asia) , Moses (Judeo-Christian), Merlin (Celtic-United Kingdom), Melchizedek (Judaism; New-Age), Babaji (Himalaya).

Strangely enough, what we know about Jesus of Nazareth comes mostly from the Gospel and the letters of Paul in the New Testament. Most accounts are based on second or third-hand information passed down through time. I read a multitude of books relating to the lost years of Jesus, which he spent in India studying and learning from other cultures' ancient mysteries. I was shocked and dismayed at how the Catholic Church had suppressed and annihilated those societies who were attempting to bring to light the real truth about Jesus Christ and Mary Magdalene and Christ's life.

I read many books about secret teachings – these documents that remained hidden and protected by the secret societies – from the Knights Templar to the Gnostics. When I read *The Templar Revelation – Secret Guardians of the True Identity of Christ,* I got an "ah-hah" moment. I always felt that what the Catholic Church had been teaching throughout my childhood didn't make sense. Something didn't feel right.

Of course, it is hard to prove if any of these documents are all really true. But I do know that Jesus came to earth, walked among us, and gave us a very simple message, which many tried to change or modify to suit their own agenda. But the truth keeps resurfacing -Jesus was real and his divinity was real. He did not come to die for our sins – he came to teach us and give us the knowledge of our all-loving Creator. Sadly enough, I was one of many who were led to focus on a bleeding and bloody figure handing on a cross – not the good works or the miracles. I was particularly interested in Jesus' approach to healing and his teachings on love and forgiveness from a non-judgmental all-loving God.

From that day on, I wore a cross in honor of Jesus and always called upon him before every Reiki healing session, as he is believed to be the head of the Great White Brotherhood, a committee of great spiritual teachers and healers overseeing the spiritual renaissance on the planet. I now focus on the Jesus who lives on in joy and happiness and always walks with us, offering help on our journey.

Now, that is something I can identify with and I honor the cross as my Master symbol in all healing sessions. Through his unconditional love, Jesus can help heal someone plagued by depression, guilt, and fear. Here is what I do before every healing session:

"I picture Jesus standing in front of me, healthy and smiling. I pour out all the love for him that I can feel,

Healing Practice and Spiritual Growth   199

sending that love to him on every deep breath that I take. (You can actually feel that love being returned to you.)

I tell him how much I love him, and that I need him today in a special way. I then tell Jesus what is on my mind and in my heart, even the deepest, darkest secrets. Ask him to help you manifest your desires, to intervene on your behalf and to give you direction on how to proceed to heal the present situation. Leave it in his loving hands, trust and allow him to work directly with God for whatever outcome is for the good and benefit of all. I love you, I thank you, and I let go of all expectations."

On the last day of the Reiki, Level III Master/Teacher training, Cheryl, our teacher, came to me and said, "I had a vision of you last night. You have many books that need to be written. You have a story to tell, and it needs to be told to help many people with their healing, to give them hope."

I replied, "Me, write a book? I don't know how to write a book. What do I write about?" I was totally puzzled.

She answered, "Meditate and ask for guidance. You will know what to do."

From that moment on, I started working on this book, working through some of my journals and working on some sections from memory. Some days, I would wake up and, almost as a sleepwalker, go to my computer, and start writing down the messages that had come to me in the night. I had so many notes that it became overwhelming. Then, it came to me that I needed to split it up into three books. This is book one.

Was it easy? Definitely not. Book writing is not for the timid. One needs to be patient, persistent, and confident in self. It took me eight years to compete the first book. Some years, especially the early years after my divorce, it was too painful to write about events that had occurred, so I would put the book away, not touching it for months on end.

Eventually, something or someone would prod me into going back to it. And so, I persisted, and somehow kept going.

SPIRITUAL GUIDES

Who are they, what do they do?
Where do they come from, are they for me and you?
What do they look like, how do they sound?
Where do you keep them, where are they found?
Can you hear them, see them, touch them
How long do they stay?
Maybe a year, a week or just even a day
Questions you ask of them you see
They are here to help us you and me
To guide and love us through all our years
Keeping away darkness and negative fears
But to find one yourself there's little to do
Just relax and listen to the true you
The little word or thought in your head
Is it a guide or something you read
My guess is with little effort and care
You're going on a journey so be prepared
To a wonderful place that's hard to have foreseen
Where your guides are and have always been
Talk to them and listen with ease
To what they say you will be pleased

© *Terrie Brushette*

CHAPTER 22

Spirit Guides

What is a Spirit Guide?

Spirit Guides are people who have passed over into the next life. They have reached a high spiritual level but still retain an interest in what is going on in the world. They are not like guardian angels that protect us, but are there to help and guide us when we ask for advice.

Guides are principally concerned with our spiritual growth and are prepared to help us with it. They want us to be independent and stand on our own two feet; therefore, they discourage us from asking for help every time we have a small problem. They prefer to act as mentors who have already learned the lessons we are so painfully trying to master. Communicate with your guides as often as you wish, but ask for help only when it is really necessary.

Your guides do not offer advice unless you ask for it. That is why some people go through their entire lives without ever realizing that they have spirit guides. Often they have not even heard of them, let alone learned how to ask their guides for help.

However, even in these cases, their spirit guides will do all they can to help them as they travel through life. In fact, if someone is in dire straits, and calls out for help, God's help will come immediately from the person's spirit guide.

Guides are discarnate entities that have not been incarnated on this plane of existence. The only exception to this rule is if someone in your family has crossed over and has attained permission to be a spiritual guide for you. Usually there are seven guides assigned to you at birth. They remain with you throughout your entire lifetime to help you fulfill your contract.

At certain times in your life, other spiritual guides will join your lifetime guides to help you work through certain issues. These can be past life issues that need to be resolved. An example would be if you became interested in healing. You would then attract healing guides or possibly fifth level surgeons that would work closely with you to teach and assist you. Another example would be if you were a musician and were trying to compose a particular piece of music. You would attract musical guides to help you.

There are certain times when we are attracted to certain cultures. It is usually due to a past life event that we have experienced. A guide may have a lot to do with that experience as well.

Angels are not guides; they are from a different realm entirely. Guides may come from other planets and are highly spiritual, evolved intergalactic beings. Be careful when you channel! Many people are channelling what they believe to be pure energy, but are not. You can tell the difference. True guides act only out of love. There is no anger, hatred or fear.

If you have never seen or spoken to your spirit guide here is one method you can use to contact them. It's called Automatic Writing.

It is essential to be relaxed when you wish to experiment with automatic writing. Sit somewhere comfortable with your writing arm creating a ninety-degree angle at the elbow. The hand holding the pen should be comfortably resting on the paper. Some people have better results using the hand they do not normally write with. Try using the other hand to see what happens.

Remain relaxed and simply wait and see what happens. Many people prefer to have their eyes closed at this stage, and go into a meditative state. After a while the hand holding the writing implement will start to move. Resist the temptation to look at what is happening, or even to show any interest. Automatic Writing is unconscious writing and any conscious interest will destroy the spontaneity and flow of the writing.

You may be fortunate and find that you start writing words and sentences from the onset. You may even write some words or phrases in mirror writing. It makes no difference what your hand draws or writes. As long as it creates something, you have made a good start.

However, you will find that on occasion, nothing is produced, even after you have been doing it successfully for several months. Do not worry about this. It simply means that nothing is available to come through at that time. Simply try again on another occasion.

Practice regularly and you will be amazed at what you produce. You will quickly discover that it is truly "automatic" and your hand is impelled by an outside force that works better when your conscious mind is out of the way.

You will also discover that you can write in this manner for hours without becoming physically tired. The writing you produce can be almost anything. You might create poems, novels, answers to questions that are troubling you or spiritual insights.

Do not evaluate anything while it is being produced. Simply record it. You can make time to evaluate and question afterwards. You will find Automatic Writing becoming more and more useful to you as time goes by. You will receive answers to questions and problems that have been bothering you. You will receive insights that will enhance your spiritual awareness, and you will be able to help others by using your automatic writing skills to answer their questions.

Many people have told me that they have learned a great deal from me and my "seminars and life stories". This is very gratifying, as I know it is only through God and my Spirit Guides that I receive these inspirations. I thank God and my Guides for my words of wisdom, not me. Yes, I am forever indebted to report to a Higher Authority in this realm and throughout my life's journey, as it is He who gave me my ability to write and resurrected my creative and analytical thought through sincere prayer. While the world revolves and humanity evolves, may we find time to be kind while we resolve our chaos and unhappiness.

You can also grow from this introspective, awakening aware-ness, mental clarity and soul-sustained experience, as I have come to realize through past-life regression, whose outcome for me has fostered a higher self-respect and understanding. As have a good lot of you, I have experienced tremendous joy and pain during the course of my life. I find it extremely therapeutic to "quill at will" about my life experiences. I have gained maturity and insight from this autobiographical writing endeavour, as well as from the private healings and seminars that I have given. I must express that I have discovered spiritual win from my journey within.

Looking back over the past years, where this journey has taken me so far, I am amazed what has come into my life, once I started trusting in a higher power and letting go of my fears...once I started to trust and work with the "Power of Three." I realized that it is okay to ask for financial assistance.

As spirit does not understand "money" as such, use the term, "abundance of financial energy." The Universe is made up of energy and abundance...and so, use those terms. Instead of thinking or saying: "I don't deserve this," say, I deserve this, and more. Thank you, God! Always end with, "This, I ask, For the Good and Benefit of all".

I guess that spirit was always with me, as they are with all of us. However, they will not interfere, until we ask for their help. An example that I was using this principle unconsciously is this: I remember when I wanted to become Regional Manager. There were no women Regional Managers in our Company at the time. Nevertheless, I persisted. I took all the management courses that I could, I told my Regional Vice-President that I wanted to become Regional Manager, once the current one retired, and I asked him what I needed to do to get there.

I started thinking and acting as the Regional Manager. I took on projects, I headed team groups, and I did brain storming. I would visualize at night that I was sitting in the Manager's office, and think and (more importantly) feel what it would be like to be the Manager...the changes I would make, the help I would provide to the staff, the good I would do for all. I felt it so deeply inside my soul that I would vibrate with the energy as I visualized how happy everyone would be and how good a job I would do. I did this every night, for over six months, and then...guess what? I got the job!

Now, I want you to close your eyes, and take three deep calming breaths. Think about one thing you really, really want the most. That is the one thing we are going to work with right now. Ask yourself what do you really, really want to be doing. Give yourself permission to be doing the things that you really want to do, instead of doing out of duty or obligations the things that you keep doing with resentment (whether conscious or unconscious).

Visualize your receiving it. How does it make you feel? Now you have asked…what happens next? It's like mailing a letter - let it go. Do not hang on to it.   Let the Universe do its work. Do not put time limits on your requests. Universe has its own time…be patient now.

You took the first step...you asked. Now, take the next step. No one else can do it for you. No knight in shining armor will come to your rescue. However, once you start the momentum going - once you take a small step - help will come to assist and support you.

Trust that the Universe will bring you what you want/need, at the right time and at the right place. Your attitude totally affects your experience. If you absolutely need to do things you do not care for, do it out of love, not resentment, and give it up to God.

It is all about intentions. Stop feeling guilty! Give it up...let it go. If you are in pain and suffering, right now...whether it is a physical ailment or mental anguish... negotiate terms with God. Ask not to "not" have the experience, instead, ask help to get through the rough ones. Ask to shorten the time, if it is painful.

Ask to learn through joy and happiness, instead of through pain and suffering. Ask God, "If I am meant to go through this, help me learn the lesson that I need. Send me the persons who will help me through this. If possible, can you shorten the time that I need to go through this... instead of months; can you shorten it to days? From days, can you shorten it to hours? For the good and benefit of all. Thank you, God."

As well, you need to balance...giving and receiving. It is very good to receive, but you must also give back. Do random acts of kindness. Give back in other ways...your time, your attention, and your empathy.

Also, pay attention to your body. If you are exhausted...you need to pay attention, stop, and refill. Do something for yourself, to get you re-energized. Go for a walk, hug a tree, take a refreshing shower, a long relaxing bath, read a good, healing book...the choices are endless. You are worthy of paying attention to yourself. You are no good to anyone if you are run-down, sick, or exhausted.

I do this all the time...any tree I happen to encounter on my daily walks with my two dogs. We have this dog park close to where I live, where I take my dogs for unleashed walking. They know the routine. They go to the closest big tree, stop, and wait for me to hug and ask the tree for its energy, which it will give to you gladly...you, need only ask! Then, they would go to the next tree, stop and wait for me to hug the tree, and so on, until I would feel re-energized enough for us to proceed on our brisk exploration walk. I felt silly at first, doing this, but it felt so good; I decided I did not care what anyone who saw me thought about it, I just did it anyways.

Do not be afraid to try things. If it does not work, admit it and move on. You have learned from that experience; now try something else. The inventor of the light bulb had 1200 failures before he got it right! School is the only place where you are punished for your mistakes. How you learn as an adult is through experiences.

So, do not be fearful. Fear is the opposite of love. Fear blocks creativity, fear allows your ego to take over. Trust your inner voice. Ask God and the angels to guide you, then let go of fear.

Give thanks often. Count your Blessings. See good and blessings all around you.

Live consciously, and be aware...follow the path of bread. What I mean by that is this: when you take a slice of bread out, think about the path that bread took to get to you. It started out by the baker making the bread, someone packaged it, someone picked it up, put it in a truck, delivered it to the grocery store, someone stocked it on the shelf, and then someone bought it and brought it to your house.

I'm not saying that you should do this about everything you take into your hands, but it's a good thing to do, once in a while, to keep you living consciously and appreciative of everything around you.

Meditate in the morning, or pray or just sit quietly. Repeat: "God/Universe: I offer you my energy to heal this world and its people, to unite the world as one race, and to bring peace, prosperity and abundance to all that share this earth with us".

Every night, before falling asleep, say this prayer: "Father God, Mother Azna, Universal Energy, I thank you for all the blessings that have been showered upon me this day."

Find the blessings that you have experienced during the day, review them and what you have learned from them, release them in light and love to the Godhead and give thanks again.

Pay attention to your body's messages. There is an emotional issue behind every ache, pain, and disease that we carry. See the examples given in the Addendum: "Emotional Sources of Disease." Forgive yourself. Illness comes from the inability to let go of the past.

Pay attention to negative people. Stay away from them, whenever possible. When this is not possible, protect yourself. Visualize putting yourself in a dome of white light, before you encounter people you know or feel are negative. This way, you will block their attempts to "steal" your positive energy..., which is why you feel "sucked out" after being around those people.

They took your positive energy, without your consent and, instead of exchanging positive energy, which you do unconsciously, but willingly with positive people...they replaced your positive energy with their negative energy, leaving you feeling exhausted. The positive energy was "sucked out of you" unconsciously, against your will.

Pay attention to your relationships. Every relationship teaches you something. Some people are in your life for a reason or for a season, not necessarily for your whole life. There are no rights or wrongs...unless you do not learn. It is OK to let go of people who no longer "serve" you.

If you have ever experienced déjà vu moments...these are confirmations you are on the right path. Take a moment to appreciate these, shout out in joy, and celebrate. These are incredible moments. Enjoy and give thanks to God for this confirmation of your life path.

In 1999, I had asked my spirit guides and God to help me find someone to love… I wrote in my journal, about this person, and I envisioned someone who is:

- Generous of spirit
- Kind to animals
- Loves dogs
- Good sense of humor
- Free to love back
- A decent golfer
- Medium height
- In good health

- Young in body and spirit
- An old soul
- Grey/light brown hair
- Positive mental attitude
- Loves to laugh/funny/witty
- Can show/express emotions
- Touchy/feely kind of guy
- Likes new things
- Open-minded
- Reliable
- Trustworthy
- Spiritual
- Knowledgeable
- Interesting to listen to

I asked the Universe to send me where I needed to go to meet this person. I have so much love to give. I wanted to share my life with someone that I can love, who will love me as well. In my journal I asked, "Does such a person exist in this lifetime for me? Well, I'm putting it out there."

Then, I reflected back on all the relationships that I had experienced in this lifetime, and what I liked and disliked about each of those relationships. Out of that last, I asked myself, "What do I want in a relationship?" and came up with this list:

- equality, not condescending
- sharing of ideas, dreams, goals and ambitions
- someone who follows through with promises
- a dreamer...but a doer

- a "can do" positive approach to life
- an "up" person, who can deal with ups and downs in a calm way
- a joy to be around and to be with
- someone with whom to share wealth, health, and spiritual growth.

That list got me thinking about my house and what I liked and disliked about it. I decided to make a list of my ideal house, what it would have in it that I loved.

In February 1999, I made up the following list: What do I want in a house of my dreams?

- Bay window with window seats
- high vaulted ceilings
- en-suite bathroom
- walk-in closet
- fireplaces
- island kitchen, roll-out drawers
- fish pond with waterfall
- trees and terraced gardens
- tiered patios
- enclosed sun porch
- sewing and pet care facilities
- view of the mountains
- large, spacious bedrooms

- large double garage
- hardwood floors throughout
- spot lighting on walls
- grand staircase
- beautiful landscaping
- air conditioned
- big entranceway

Do not be scared to ask for what you really, really want. You don't ask...you don't get. I asked the universe for the above, only if it is meant to be, for the good and benefit of all, that I choose to feel worthy and deserving, and that I am willing to receive abundance.

When people complain that they are "so busy all the time," I tell them they are so blessed. A life filled with "busy" is a happy life, because it is blessed with so much purpose and direction. So, instead of complaining - give thanks to God for your busy life.

Only God and You really know who you are, and what your motives are. It is not about winning popularity contests. It is not about doing things for others "because I feel guilty or I have to, or I need to." It is about what you want to do ... for yourself and for others. You just have to be true to yourself. You cannot fool your heart and soul.

There are simply things we have to go through, without warning, so we can learn from them. There are no accidents. The warnings (or lack of them) were put there by you, before you came to earth. The people who have given you warnings were also put there by you, and agreed to with them, that they would be there for you at certain times in your life...whether these are (in this lifetime) family, friends, neighbors, acquaintances, psychics, guides, angels or total strangers.

Two key ingredients to real health are staying busy and helping others. Nowadays, there are so many "new" illnesses: fibromyalgia, candida, chronic fatigue syndrome; as well as all the strange viruses that are cropping up all over the planet. Remember, "What comes around goes around." Is this the planet's retaliation for all the harm that has been done to its animals, its oceans, rivers, and lakes, its atmosphere, its forests and rain forests?

Those of us who have chosen this era to come here are true warriors. We've chosen the worst era in the planet's history ... pollution, war, hatred, intolerance, injustice, poverty, abuse of children and the elderly...the list goes on and on. Take heart, as we are those who have been brave enough to come here at this time, when the planet is in a crisis. Our positive energy and "good work" will help turn it around. Stay positive and surround yourself with goodness.

You will make mistakes, just as I did. In reflecting back, however, you will see that those mistakes were really experiences or side trips... they all taught you something that brought you to where you are today. Don't beat yourself up by putting self-critical judgments about your personal life experiences.

You will continue to make mistakes and you will learn from them and do better and even make different mistakes. Reflect on them. Get the lesson you need to learn from those experiences, and "get over yourself"... move on!

If you cannot figure out what the lesson is, just give it up to God, saying, "Whatever lesson I was meant to learn from this episode/experience/mistake, please help me incorporate that lesson into my cell memory, so that I can learn and grow from it. Thank You, God."

KINDNESS

What could be greater than to realize this?
That kindness is the way to all gain and all knowing
That kindness is the only thing that ever matters
What else is there to be which takes us further
Than being kind to someone for no reason?
Other than to be kind!
Loving those around us is the only way to anything
Because there's no distinction between them and us
When we give to someone, we give to ourselves as well
Not because giving might bring us some nice reward
But because that person is us and we are them!
Not just similar to us, for that's not enough
We're each guided by the same force
And made of the very same stuff!
Kindness is our greatest gift to ourselves
Kindness is our birthright and our responsibility
Kindness is our way home
Kindness is the true religion of all the universe!

Gordon Rosenberg

CHAPTER 23

Random Acts of Kindness

March 1999

K athy and I decided to take a week's holiday and go to the Dominican Republic. In reading about the Island, I knew about the extreme poverty we would encounter there, so Kathy and I started gathering clothing and medicine cabinet stuff: Tylenol, Advil, Band-Aids, antiseptic, ointments, and so on. We also put together a kit for schoolchildren: pencils, pencil sharpeners, notebooks, toys and wrapped candies. We each spent about fifty dollars for this project.

When we got to the airport in Toronto, ready to board the chartered flight through Canada 3000, the flight coordinators at the airport told me it would cost an additional seventy-five dollars because of the additional weight for the suitcase.

I explained to them what we were taking to the Island, to help the locals. I implored them to try to get the cost lowered, so that we would be able to afford to bring stuff on our next travel. The two flight registration assistants went to a lot of trouble for me, but

they managed to waive the fee for the additional weight. I took both their names down and when I returned home a week later, I wrote to the President of Canada 3000. I told him our story and gave him the names of the two outstanding people who had gone above and beyond to help us do good for the locals in the Dominican Republic.

I actually got a response from him, acknowledging receipt of my letter, saying that he appreciated that I had taken the time to write a thank you letter. Most people do not. The occasional phone call, yes, but letters are most time-consuming, so most people do not bother. When someone does a random act of kindness, acknowledge it, somehow, if you can. If you cannot, well then, pass it on!

So, there we were in Puerto Plata, Dominican Republic. We had booked a jungle tour and talked with the driver beforehand. We asked if it would be possible to stop at a local school, as we had gifts to give. Could he find out how many kids were at the school, to ensure we had enough for the entire class?

The day of the tour came, and off we went with our packsacks full of pencils, notebooks, toys, and candy for the schoolchildren. When we got to the school, the children came out to the roadside, and Kathy and I distributed our gifts, ensuring each child received equally.

The rest of the people on the tour bus wanted to know why we were stopping. When we explained to them our mission, they all said, "Aw…why didn't we think of that? It is just such a beautiful thing to do. Well, next time we go to an island, we'll do the same." Therefore, a random act of kindness is passed on.

As we were leaving, there was a little boy, maybe 4–5 years old, walking alongside the road, so we asked the driver to stop and handed him a little toy tank truck. You should have seen his eyes light up…it brought tears to our eyes. It is a very humbling experience and I encourage all who travel to bring something from Canada to give to the locals. It is so rewarding.

We visited a farm on the Island and it was a real revelation for me. They only use their humble house for sleeping quarters. It had two bedrooms, separated by a half-wall, with no doors for privacy. There was a small table, a few chairs and some open cupboards. Their toilet facilities are outside and their bath area is the ocean. Their cooking is done in a little hut, separate from the house and barn. There were big basket containers hooked on the outside of the barn wall that the free-range chickens use as their nests. Very innovative, I thought.

Upon my return back home after that trip, I pondered on the reasons behind all the trips I had taken since my divorce and I realized that I had to see how other people lived their lives, so that I could create a new life for my "self". I also learned from the random people that I encountered on those trips. One such lesson was on our last day. We got into the resort taxi to go to the airport. We were driving in the right lane when suddenly a car jumped out of a parking space right in front of us. The taxi driver slammed on his brakes, skidded, and missed the other car by just inches!

The driver of the other car whipped his head around and started yelling at us. Our driver just smiled and waved at the person, with a big smile on his face. He wasn't upset at all, and didn't react, other than smiling. I was quite indignant myself. So I asked, 'Why did you just do that? Didn't that upset you? That other driver never looked before jumping out in our lane - he almost ruined your car and sent us to the hospital!'

What he taught me, I'll never forget and would like to pass it on to you. I can't quite remember the entire conversation, but it went something like this - many people run around full of frustration, full of anger, and full of disappointment. As their garbage piles up, they need a place to dump it and sometimes they'll dump it on you. Don't take it personally. Just smile, wave, wish them well, and move on. Don't take their garbage and spread it to other people at work, at home, or on the streets.

The bottom line is that we should not let other people's garbage take over our day. Life's too short to wake up in the morning with regrets, so... love the people who treat you right. Pray for the ones who don't. After all, life is ten percent what you make it and ninety percent how you take it!

LOOK TO SPIRIT

When you are feeling that sorrow is near,
Don't wallow in self pity, don't worry,
There's no need to fear.
Our life is a mystery of ups and downs,
Of tears and smiles, and often frowns.
Remember our loved ones in spirit
Know how we feel.
They'll bring you comfort, and hands to heal.
And lay in your path a brighter day,
With solutions to problems, that hinder your way.
Love will survive the change called death.
It will surround you like a flowers sweet breath.
Like a guardian angel, watching you sleep.
These are but memories, a reminder to keep.
To tell you that their soul has not died,
But all through your life, they'll be by your side.

Lancashire

CHAPTER 24

Beacons of Wisdom

August 1999

At this point in my life, I knew that I had taken huge leaps forward. I decided to book an appointment with a spiritual intuitive, Margaret from Winnipeg, Manitoba. This is an excerpt from that session:

"You've been gathering a lot of spiritual knowledge lately, because there's a wise soul who is a mentor to you. He is really with you, pulling in the spiritual knowledge. He says sometimes you drain yourself...you just push and push and he's concerned about that because he says you get yourself to the point where you fall asleep and you're exhausted; it's always an exhausted sleep.

He is concerned about that, because all they can do in that kind of situation is to repair your energies. He needs you to relax more. You are so spiritual in yourself and you know that. You have spirit lights all around you - good energy and an awful lot of good people working with you. Among them is your mother. When your mother passed, she was quite sick. She was old in her ways before she passed. Old in herself in that she was very, very tired. Life had been quite a struggle for her and she has not passed over that long ago. (Note: Mom had passed over in October 1998.)

Your mom is still in a sort of sense of recovery there. She is showing me you are weighing out many of your own truths; right now, many things you did not settle. She has your head in her lap, she says you have a need for a safe place and she reassures you that you are in a safe place.

Your mom says that sometimes you go where you should not, that you tend to think after the fact. Well, she's putting a lot of her energy here, and ... if you notice that lately you've rather been held back a little; you think to go somewhere within yourself, but you don't get there. However, you feel better because you did not go there...well; she is putting that energy there. It is like cool energy. To you, it is just like a feeling: "can't do that today."

Therefore, your mom wants you to go a different pathway. She says you really need to hold back more, right now, go around things and sidestep a lot. Because if you do not, you are going to trip and hurt yourself, you are going to do yourself damage.

Your brother and your grandfather are both here, now. Your brother's energy is coming over your right shoulder and down the front. Your grandfather's energy is going from the left shoulder away from the body. Your grandfather says to wait off on a decision right now. They are re-directing you. Your brother was quite a spirited young man, wasn't he? Happy, and had a good attitude, and then he died quite suddenly... he was like...gone, just like that!

There is someone quite close to you on earth, another brother. He has been growing a lot in intellectual and spiritual understanding, lately. He is getting a lot of knowledge from spirit right now, and its showing. He still has not dealt with something ...the death of your mother. More than the others, she was more concerned about him. She says he is coming together quite well right now. He is on a new pathway; the spirits are really working with him as well. You give him a lot of space and this is wise on your part. But you listen, and in the listening, you have both grown.

Your grandfather is saying you need some laughter in your life, as you have not had as much lately. He says you have to find the bright spots again, because for the last 3-4 years, your life has been in turmoil. The divorce was not a bad move...ultimately; it was a good move. Now you are really coming into your own reality. You are rooted in yourself. You are starting to feel more centered. Work issues have been good. You are good with business... good business acumen.

Your grandfather is with someone whose hands shake a lot. Note: my dad had a stroke, which has left him with a very shaky right hand). He is with him often. They are really with him in the energies...when you see him sort of spaced out; what they are doing is taking him a lot to the spirit world. So, if he seems to be "not there, vague sometimes", its okay. He is going to be here (on earth) for a while yet; he is not leaving yet. From their end, they say he seems to need to be here.

You have a big family. (Note: mom and dad had a family of twelve; six boys and six girls. One boy passed over at age 10.) One sister...she is very different from the rest of you. She just seems to have a completely different understanding; she is very spiritual. She is very, very strong. I see gold here ... all spirit light. She does not really bend at all, and she is very meaningful in your life. The spirits work with her a lot. Your other sisters come and go; they do not have the same value system. One starts here; one goes there... preoccupied, going off in different directions, but not grounded. Their lives are fine, but they do not have the awareness that this one sister has. The two of you were always close, but not like now. She works with the angel realm; you know...she really does. I do not see that often, but there are angels here, and she knows truth with such clarity, and she actually got you centered. She is a resilient woman, and yet she has had her own hardships. She calls them "good ships" - her attitude is so good.

Another of your brothers is not well, his health is not that great; it is in the upper part of him. He keeps to himself, but he is at peace in his own way. You often put prayer petition out for him, and its working. Sometimes, you don't see it on the earth plane, but you have to know it on the spiritual plane, all right?

At work, sometimes you are trying to figure out how to put something into place; the spirits are with you on that. It will come from within. You have a natural ability to go with the flow, and you connect with people quite easily. They always seem to grasp your presentations and very often, people will talk to you after, because you have clarity about you. It is because you work with an energy field, and you do it very well, so spirit is saying not to worry about that aspect of your life. Your boss at work, he thinks highly of you, and he actually has given you a lot of direction himself, hasn't he? He is a nice man. I like his energies and he has given you the support that you have sometimes needed. He is not very old. However, he was meant to come into your pathway and he has helped you to understand your difficulties. He understands the cross you have borne, so he is aware and openhearted to you, and that is important.

There is someone else now...who likes fishing a lot. His wife just passed over this morning. He was expecting it, and he helped her release herself. There is a mother or grandmother on the other side, they are there to greet her, and she is on her way. She is fine. There is a celebration for her over there...because I just saw the spirit bell – that's pretty. There are good energies there; the healing has begun for her. Your friend's energy will be quite low for some time, because he gave a lot of himself, so it will take time. Tell him he needs to be walking, he needs to be outside, because they want to rebuild his energies right now, before the fall; it will be a bit of a hard winter.

With your son - you two are very close. You've been together in many lifetimes. You have a special bond."

I see a woman…she was very tiny when she was young, an aunt always fussing with her hair. Didn't know her that well, did you? I see her bending over to a flower garden, to the rose. Her name is Rose…you were named after her. (She is my godmother). She is giving you a big hug. She is straightening you out, in a loving way. She's turning your around, saying, "Let's get on with it." She has a lot of love for you.

She is really a character. She's serious one minute, full of fun the next. She says she loves your hair. Hair was a thing with her. Yours is cute; I really like the new look...very youthful. You have come alive, and she is very pleased with that. She sometimes helps you wash your hair.

Your bedroom...what is going on with your dresser? Some family jewelry? Long pieces? Your mom's jewelry...clean it and wear it. A silver piece - she wants you to wear it for her. It is a nice piece. That would be very healing for you. Your mom, she is fine over there. She rather likes it. She says it's neat. She was not expecting what she saw. She is looking around. There was a child that passed on. They are having a good time together. She is happy. He comes and he stays with her. He is showing himself to her young right now because she would have a little trouble with the concept. Therefore, she is quite excited that she found him. He is slowly going to give her the understanding. She likes to pat his head; she is pleased. She was a very patient woman, she does not quite understand. She is not sure of her new body; she still thinks she is in her old body, so that is limiting her, but the spirits are working with her on this.

They are giving her the concept that she can now wander around; she is just getting to that stage. Your brother is there, and it happened that the way they had to do this was introduce it to her as a memory. Then - make it a reality, because she would be too overwhelmed otherwise. . Therefore, they work in a dream state. She is doing her handwork, then she sees him, and she is quite happy. In the next six months or so, you will find yourself in a church somewhere, do not plan it, it will just happen. Light a candle for you and her. It will give her a step.

A girlfriend who is quite chatty, but not quite expressing herself. High energy, but not listening well. You try to be clear with her, but she does not want to hear truth. She's very frightened, this woman. She brings hardships onto herself; she keeps dropping herself into these nightmares, gets into such darkness. You have been so good to her; it is helping you to grow. As you work with her, you clear up your own garbage. When you give, you receive. You have not known her really well for that long, just a couple of years. Light a candle for her, when she crosses your mind. It needs to be a blue candle. Always imagine her energies are open to the universe. See her crown opening to the universe. They cannot connect to her, because she is not open, although they are trying. She is a good, hard worker and she does a good job. Give her a couple of books, and write a nice inspiration, don't plan it, just do it.

A family member where there is surgery coming up. The surgeon is good. There is a scare of something, but when I see the tunnel, it is green and it is not complete. They feel they're going to pass, but they're not.

A white toy poodle here belongs to one of your friends. She needs to know that it's all right. She's fine. (Note: my friend from Regina, Saskatchewan, Melody Jones, a month before this reading, had her toy poodle pass over.) She used to put ribbons on her; she has pink ribbons on. She was a confident little dog. She's just perky, had a great personality. She was just sitting there. She's fine.

You have a protector, too. Four feathers is his name. I just saw him. He has red feathers, and he likes rawhide. If you ever smell leather, that's because of him. That's his connection. So, when you smell leather, or think of leather, pay attention to what's going on in your life at that time, because he's giving you truth. So, be aware, not to analyze, but pay attention to your self-development at that point, because he's coming in there to give you enlightenment.

He's an old spirit, and he's smoking a pipe in the house... he's blowing smoke rings on the house. He has a sense of humor, too. He's pointing to your brother. You're affecting your brother who's living with you, and he doesn't really realize it, right? He (four feathers) is having fun with this. He's pointing and saying, "We're getting places, with your brother." You are getting places with your brother. Is your brother going to move on? Is there talk of moving on? By the spring, something comes up in his life that changes his life. He seems to... he's helping someone right now that is very ill, but she is very accepting of that.

You have a problem with your insides. You need to go for therapeutic massage, maybe once a month. You have to bath with Aromatherapy and massage your stomach area. When you do that, envision the healing pulling out the fibroids. In the spirit world, they are saying that fibroids are just a natural part of the change that doctors don't totally understand...are just energy change s which create energy builds and then they pass after, and so it's not necessary to panic about them. There doesn't appear to be any danger. It's all blue, and it's all healing in there...there's no red spots or hot spots, or that looks frightening. They want you to make sure you massage under your arms, it's important you don't wear bras as much as possible. A spot there could cause a blockage, so just massage or just put your hands there and press. There has to be a healing there that has to be looked after.

You're not moving back to the mountains...for a long while. Because your lessons are here...you need the lessons here. In the third year you're here, you are going to be happy - sometime into 2002. Something is going to take place in your life, and you're going to say, "Well, if I wouldn't have been here..."You will have the realization of why you really needed to be here. In five to seven years, you may have the opportunity to move back; it may not be your choice to do so. Do not start a bed and breakfast operation; you need to spend this next year on doing your spiritual work.

You're not destined to be alone, but you need to be alone now. You're never alone, but I see a partnership with a very gentle soul. Not now - much later. He's not on your pathway for a while. However, the experiences lead you to a good understanding, you need grounding, but you need someone who can appreciate your energy field. You can keep a man young; you have that ability...to keep someone young. This man seems to be older, but you bring him younger. What you share together is very special. It's what you share with him... he just opens up your vision to a different kind of beauty and peace, but it's down the path, you don't know him yet.

However, you need this other area of development for yourself. It will come good. You're a go-getter. You're not a person to stop. You still need a couple of good cries. There are a couple of things you haven't totally let go of yet, but really just let it out. You just need a release. It's sort of: "This can't happen before that happens." There's crying and there is wailing, and you've already done that. I see that spongy heart coming into place, and then it has formed, shaped, and ready to go. Right now, it could be damaged, because there is a part of your emotional sense that's not centered yet, and so you need to understand that...spirit is releasing the pressure

Furthermore, you're going to the USA...you're going south. Look forward to a very positive experience there. You've had a past life there. This will be connectiveness and a spiritual experience. You did live there, the belle of the ball. You've called yourself jokingly...a Cajun queen, but it's a reality. You did live in that time. This is good, because you had a very happy life there. (Author's note: The Company I worked for sent me to New Orleans in February 2000, for a Marketing Conference. I visited a plantation home where I truly felt I had been there before.)

End of transmission.

ENCOURAGEMENTS

We are not human beings
on a spiritual journey;
we are spiritual beings
on a human journey.

Kimi Mulero

CHAPTER 25

More Divine Guidance

May 2000

I had a Celtic Cross Tarot Card Reading. My question was, "Give me guidance about my love life and how conditions will progress over the next three to six months."

This is the spread used in such a reading:

1. YOU: represents your place in the situation and what you need to do to realize upper innermost desires:

   Card: Seven of Pentacles – Frustration: You need to cope with frustration. If hard work has not paid off as you planned, remember that expectations are always unreasonable. There are no guarantees. Be grateful. Focus on the present. Do what you can with what you have.

2. WHAT SURROUNDS YOU: represents the conditions surrounding you regarding the question. If answer is harmonious, then you are in a supportive position.

Card: Princess of Wands – Impulsiveness: You are surrounded by spontaneity and enthusiasm, which may turn to impatience, anger, and theatrics if control is lost. News of an opportunity is near. A blunt, fiery, or impulsive person may help or need help.

3. WHAT BLOCKS YOU: What imbalance may prevent you from achieving the outcomes indicated in #7 (Truth) and #11 (Dynamism). It also represents what is confusing to you.

    Card: Ten of Pentacles – Protection: Protection or lack of it, blocks your progress. Too much… you are kept from life lessons. Too little…You are wounded and must heal. A well-known name or reputation can be a curse. An over-protective person or relative may be the problem.

4. YOUR FOUNDATION: represents a fundamental issue, which can give you strength and security necessary to accomplish your goal.

    Card: Seven of Wands – Courage: Crucial to your situation is courage. It is vital to go forward in spite of your fears. You may need to go it alone. Come out from behind your defenses and act.

5. WHAT IS BEHIND YOU: Past actions and influences, which have brought things to be the way, they are now. Also represents ideas and conditions that are passing out of your life.

    Card: Temperance – Patience: The time of patience, mixing and waiting has passed. If this time was used well, all is prepared for effective action. If time was wasted, stop complaining. You must stop, look, and listen before you act.

6. WHAT CROWNS YOU: represents the spiritual goal you must work towards in order to attain what you desire. It contains a visualization exercise to help you do so.

    Card: Eight of Pentacles - Craftsmanship: Deal with your situation as a skilled crafts person would. Visualize each element of your situation as a brick that you examine closely as you build your home. Be a skilled mason and live well.

7. WHAT IS BEFORE YOU: Conditions you will encounter in the near-term future ...next 3 to 6 weeks.

    Card: Justice - Truth: You will soon get what you deserve. Agreements may be made and upheld. There may be a re balancing on all levels, including financial and legal. Truth and Justice will prevail. Your life will be beautified in some ways.

8. HOW TO PRESENT YOURSELF: How you should best conduct yourself in order to achieve your goal. Do so knowing there is a risk that others may misinterpret your actions.

    Card: Five of Pentacles – Anxiety: Present yourself as having to cope with stress and anxiety. Let others know you are at a difficult time in your life. It is not weakness, but the greatest strength to ask for their help. If they avoid you - move on and find out who your real friends are.

9. HOW OTHERS SEE YOU: How people important to your situation see you in relation to the question. It may be different from #8 above.

    Card: Princess of Pentacles – Practicality: Others see you as concerned with the communication of practical information and useful techniques. You seem to enjoy getting your hands dirty and the sweat of honest labor. Some may think you move too slowly.

10. YOUR HOPES AND FEARS: Deep-seated fear you have that you may not be aware of. Represents hopes and fears you have about the way your life will change when you attain your goal.

    Card: The Hanged Man – Suspension: You hope to take the time out of your everyday life to look at things from a different perspective but fear you will still feel restricted no matter what you do, say or think. You may fear being suspended or trapped. You may fear heights.

11. THE OUTCOME: Conditions you can expect to encounter in the next three to six months.

    Card: King of Wands – Dynamism. You will encounter or have to act as a dynamic, dominant person who is absolutely sure she is right. Decisive action will be taken. Loyalty will be rewarded.

Later that November, during a meditation, I asked myself, "What does Estelle really, really want? For the benefit of my higher self?" Family has always been very important to me. Therefore, I asked to be close to my family, especially my kids and grandkids…to help them grow and remember their spirit. I asked to attract to me friends with whom we can help each other in remembering our spirit. I asked for help to be able to afford to quit. I asked for a buy-out package to start a very, very successful healing business, and the financial freedom to help others. I asked to stay fit and healthy.

In addition, for my house, I asked to finish a suite on the lower level and get a Jacuzzi tub. As far as companionship is concerned, I knew I was seeking a relationship with a suitable mate…to grow to love and appreciate each other, living in complete harmony. For my soul, I asked for guidance to go within, to remember my spirit, to learn what I need to learn on this journey.

April 2001

It now had been two years since my last visit with the Winnipeg spiritual intuitive, Margaret. Therefore, I booked another session with her for April 3, 2001. The following are excerpts from that taped session.

"There are different things going on with your energy. You are a little out of balance lately. You have been feeling low on energy, your aura is out of balance, and it is sort of pulling on you. You can't get centered. There is a nun here; she's been here twice already. You've been going into spirit a lot lately. You need to get to sleep quickly. She's been taking you to a foreign country, doing rescue work, where there are many hidden messages. You see a lot of suffering. As a result, when you wake up, you feel very heavy-hearted, and you can't quite figure it out. She herself finds it...you know when you go through a war... as you did in a past life. You go through and you're learning things quickly, but you can't stay, for fear of being known. So, that's very intriguing. You feel like you belong, but you don't belong, right now.

It's a really odd thing. You're functioning on the outside of yourself, but on the inside, many things are mixing up inside yourself, and you can't get it straight. But, you're learning. All they're giving me is - it's a preparation. You're doing very good work. Do you get an odd pull in your stomach...like a stomachache? It's a different energy field that they're using that I have not seen before; it's a female energy that's just coming into the planet. That's a new one! They're drawing on it. You know the root chakra. But it's not, it's different. It has spiritual energy in it. They put it into place, and they've got it going.

There's a Father Esau, here. There's an older man that you keep getting a feeling of. He's coming in. Do you do chanting? A form of affirmation? Has your form of affirmation been changing? When you try, it's a view...when you listen, its right. That's what you're doing. You feel like you want to say something, but you can't quite understand what it is. This Father Esau is here, and he's schooling you, so ...you don't feel your affirmations right now...it's like saying them, but they're empty.

Because you haven't reached that bounce of energy in which to really get to the heart. You keep a hold back on your heart, anyway. You really are careful with your heart. It's like" No, I won't open it, because if I do..." You'd rather remain curious to people. You like to keep an air about you. Yet, you're observing at the same time. You look like you're doing something, but very inconspicuously, you're gleaning knowledge. You don't even know you're doing it. It's as if you're preoccupied with something else, but yet, you're picking up (learning) the understanding of the energy fields around you, and you're finding a lot of sadness there lately.

This is a lot of spirit work; this is very different. You pulling away from people, lately...you can't be bothered. It really doesn't matter, anymore, so you're letting a lot of people fall away. You're more interested in knowledge and learning in your own space and time. It's like refining ... you're learning to differentiate spiritual values. For a long time, you gave too much of yourself, and you were misunderstood. Things are starting to come to you. Don't go off your own track.

Stay in your truth of conviction. Something could look just as appealing, and when you turn around, it would be the opposite of what you knew, but it would be so close to it, that you could be deceived. You need to stay facing towards the sun.

You work better in sun energies. Sun energies aren't as common as moon energies...a lot of people work more in moon energies. But you definitely work better in sun energies. And so, you really need this rejuvenation time.

Your son...he's quite a determined man, isn't he? You're doing what you need to be doing, and he's out there doing what he needs to be doing. However, you're now starting to pull closer.

Your grandson. (Author's note: Mathew. He's five years old). You need to be spending time with him. He has very healing hands. He plays with energy. He does short different things with his hands...a sort of choppy thing. He has a different energy. He has big hands. What he has to learn is... he plays with a dog...one animal particularly. (Author's note: My dog, Skippy). Help him to learn to feel energy from the animals. This animal, particularly. Get him to feel and play with the energy. He has the gift, but he needs to do a lot of earning between five and seven, because there is different energy coming. He needs to learn about energy. Teach him in game ways, particularly with this dog. He really loves this dog. He puts his head to him, or his ear. He's sensing energy.

Children do things, but not by chance. None of us do, but he does not understand. He hears energy, too. He hears funny things. (Author's note: Mathew would ask to go upstairs, get on my Reiki table, and ask me to put my hands on him for a few minutes, then he's say: "That's enough, Nana." and get up and go on playing as before.) People are going to be able to hear energy.

Spirit wants to say, "You know the Northern Lights? Some people can hear that energy, but can't record it, yet, because they don't know the vibrations." And that's really something important for Mathew. He hears the energy. It's important for you to make sure...so, sound is going to be his field... he must be very sensitive to sound. He will be, you watch! You watch his eyes. He'll hear, but you'll see that he's hearing with his eyes. He's very close with his father. There is quite an energy connection there, more so than the other one. The other one is younger...around three. However, this one...he is very much closer with his father, right now.

Is his mother away...in herself? She appears preoccupied. It's really, really, important, because he needs to be connected. She seems like a very gentle woman. I really like her energy...very soft, very soft-spoken, and very loving. She's a sweetheart, but she lost some period in her life, and she's making up for it now. Spirit is saying that it's really, important that she gets her space.

Your son is looking to advance himself, into something a little different. You know how sometimes you go backwards to get something, and then when you go to pick it up, something else catches your eye? I don't know if that means he's taking a couple of steps backwards, in a sense. But he's going to notice something on the earth that's going to give him a new sense of direction, and more challenging - from the material to a spiritual understanding of the material. And when you get that, then things work better.

Your son did have a difficult time there for a bit. It was as if everything was going backwards instead of going forward. But then it smoothed itself out. It won't go back like that again, but now it's like, "Good, he's done his homework and now there are rewards at the end of the tunnel." 'Cause he is an achiever, your son. He is very bright, in a nice way...not pushy with people. Really teases well with you. He's being very gentle with you.

Who passed over with congestive heart failure or upper respiratory problems? This is a man. Was your grandfather close with you? He is here. He says you're learning to speak differently. You are starting to speak your truth. It's coming easier. You say less, but it means more. He says, "I've been working with you." He was the kind that looked around...that would view life.

He's saying to you, "Look around, really look good. There's a greener pasture there for you. I'm going to help you, because you don't quite have it in your vision...you see it, but you don't." It has to do with little pasture of learning...something that you haven't seen out there that's very positive for you. He's going to get your attention on it, and you're going to be drawn to it. Going into something unreal, but it becomes real, and when you come back, it clears your view. It's on the earth plateau. Therefore, he's going to make you aware of it. This doesn't happen until later.

Have you felt your mother around you, lately? Your mother is in spirit. You look like your mother. She used to draw her brow in. That's what she's doing right now. She keeps giving you love; because you really let her go when she passed...you released her. She says that was really good, because now she can really come back in her full essence, spiritually. She's talking about one of your sisters... one that she was closer to. Because she says, "Have you been in touch with her? Do you talk to her, clearly? It's time. Speak plainly anymore. It's as if...she seems that she looks around at things, she won't settle. She looks quite nervous, agitated. Does she have heart trouble, or chest trouble? Something here is showing itself in the chest cavity. There is something that she needs to check out."

She was hurt a lot in her life. It's as if I see many daggers going in, and she's taken about as much as she can. Sometimes, there could be a cause and effect, so it's a good idea for her to pay attention to her health. Your mother is nodding and saying, "Yes, point her in the right direction, at the right time." Your mother wasn't one to be that outspoken. She was more in the sense of giving direction, more like a nudge, gently. However, if you were smart, you'd catch on. So, that's what she's doing right now.

Then your other sisters are neither here, nor there. They live, but they don't. Moreover, that's the way it's going to stay. So, in a sense, there are only three of you sisters. You lost a brother. He's been here before. He's a bit of a character. He's clearing the way for you. He says, "Let the other ones be who they are. It doesn't really much matter. The focus is on the three of you. It's truly important, that you learn how to shovel out the garbage." You are learning to set boundaries...how to separate and divide. In other words, like Moses, you're learning to separate the waters. You are learning; now, to walk in your own truth and this is very, very important. Your brother's there being a bit of a card, 'because he says you're starting to find humor back again.

You spend a lot of time with one friend in particular. Is that person distancing herself? This is a very close friend who's going out there to become more knowledgeable. She's an intellect. She'll have to do her own thing for a while, and that's okay with you, but you're sad about it. Be happy for her. She really needs to do this thing. Its part of what she has to complete.

Your mother's energy is back. She's saying, "When you lose something, you feel a sense of emptiness. She says don't. She'll fill it." Your mother says you used to love the beach. You used to play with a beach ball. She says you need to go back into that part of yourself. The beach would be good for you. Recount the memories of the beach, the time where you really stayed centered.

You were in your own universe for a while, and that was really important. You need to do that again.

There are courses at work you're going to take...spirit is slipping in a little spiritual schooling from a work ethic. You're going to chuckle and think, "If they knew what they were teaching, or showing, they probably wouldn't do it." It's going to make you laugh. The instructor is going to be unknowing of what they are instructing. This is the earth schooling, but it will end up being a spiritual experience.

You're going on a trip - by plane. This is a must. You're going to have many positive results from this trip. It's a short trip...seven to ten days. This is with a girlfriend you haven't seen for a while. You're both going in different pathways. Yet, very each content in your own. You're two very individual people.

She's in a curve; right now, she's coming out into something new in herself. She did this well. She actually didn't force anything, and it's good. She should know she's on track. When you get together, it's very powerful. You always reinstate one another. She has a good head. I like this girl. She gets absentminded...she's scratching her head. She's so preoccupied, because she doesn't know how to do it any other way; she's like an overachiever. You haven't had a good chin-wagging in a long time, and it's time. You may even get her full attention, this time!

Your partner from five years ago...he's gone. You're finished with that relationship. He still bothers you, but he's changing...becoming more distant. This is good. It had to happen. It feels like its just dissipating. This new person you're seeing right now, he has very different ideas. He makes you think a lot. You don't always agree quite easily with him. It's like seeing an "s" trail with him. You go around this way to come into this other way. You're not really connected to him...I don't think so! He's not for you. He's not your cup of tea. He's unclear with you, he tells you part of something, but doesn't give you the whole picture. This gets you frustrated and then you let it go. You think, "That's not fair...why are you pulling this?" Therefore, he won't give you a real sense of himself. He's evasive - that's him.

It's not a connection of the heart. You're asking yourself, "How long do I do this?" It's not connectiveness in the right way for you. It's making you distance what you know of yourself. That's too much compromise. In one way, he has intelligence. You have learned to look at things differently. It's made you have a different approach to how you hear things. He didn't learn - he doesn't know how to put it together. He did the same thing to his wife, because he doesn't know how to be with a woman. It's not something you can teach a man.

Your aunt Rose...a bit of a go-getter. She was a very determined woman. She says to you, "We're outa here...get on your bike and cycle away. There are better things to do with your life." You're weaning this relationship anyways. You don't have to do anything to end this relationship; the universe will do it for you. Just go with the flow, and don't beat yourself up about it. You're somewhat amazed at how you can't connect lately, how it's pulling away on its own. He's sort of an empty person...empty for your needs. He's not your type. He's not open to spiritual things, and you can't explain it to him...don't bother. It would fall on deaf ears, don't even go there. He doesn't get the concept.

Your aunt... she's funny. She's a character herself, a real gutsy girl. She says, "I'm going to teach you to go uphill...this is good stuff. You've got more than you think you've got, you've got what it takes." You're discovering yourself, and so you haven't noticed that lately.

Boss at work...a male – he draws you into situations, then all of a sudden, you have a surprise. Watch out. You don't like it. This is one time they're asking you to go back and observe. There is a routine, a system here, where you are drawn in. There's a point where you have a point of exit, where you can be gracious but not get caught up in it. Every time, you do, you really get annoyed with yourself because you get loaded down, and you're thinking, "How did this happen to me? I wasn't planning on this!" You have to go back and see, just remember each time, where you had a choice and you didn't make it. A choice isn't really a conscious: "I have a choice." Rather, it's a turning point where you're saying: "Wait a minute, I can alter this."

Someone is coming up in the ranks. It's a good person. Whoever it is would be spiritual. Your boss, who has been there for a few years...he doesn't quite fit in. Spirit is showing that he's going to "get bumped"... up or out. Sometimes, people are smooth, but they're not. He appears smooth, but he's not. He's good at manipulating things, but they have another soul coming in. When that happens, it will be better. Someone is coming from elsewhere... another department? Fresh air comes with it. This is good.

Still like your aunt. She's a bit of a character. She's back again. She's just a gutsy girl. She is funny. She says when you hear ringing in your ears...that's her. She says when that happens, pay attention. In school, you would always read everything and take it in. Just stay in that way of yourself, that's important.

Energies are changing in your hands. When you go over in spirit...when they take you over in spirit, it's like a steam bath for your hands, changing the energy fields. Your hands must be feeling differently, lately. They feel full, but yet not completed. That's what they're doing. They're working a different energy. When you work with healing, do you use the tips of your hands? You're feeling drawn to go more to the tips...why aren't you doing that, they're saying. Because you come in from a sort of an angle and, that's the way you have to, otherwise you don't deliver the energy correctly. Sometimes your energy backs up inside you.

So they're saying. You keep flowers in the house. You need mauve ones. You need that energy. It's important for you to fuss with the flowers, because flowers give out something, and they say it'll balance you. Lilacs...keep many bouquets. Your mother used to have lots of them, also.

You've been having problems with your back, in the lower part. Lay on a heating pad (not an electric pad), lay, relax, and do deep breathing. You're not working it right, trying too hard. Just relax and find your own natural flow. You don't adhere to what you think you should know you adhere to what you feel. You catch a funny energy in there; put something under your knees. Just lay and burn two white candles, one on each side of the bed.

The energies will start to build, and finally meeting and joining. It's also the energy in your bedroom. It hasn't been right. It's a little messed up. It's as if you have two levels of energy. What happened in there? It wasn't always like this. Light your two white candles on both sides of the bed. They will join, and you will feel the energy as if you're in a hammock.

Did you ever get a woman that comes, she wears a veil - but not East Indian, Her name is Anya. She says, "Why don't you be silent when you want to be?" She is very loving, this one. Your mother knows her; obviously, cause here comes your mother again. She says, "Just, you know, that veil, it's no sense to put your truth out, it makes you feel like you have to explain. There is no sense in your trying to explain. Just pretend that I've put the veil across you, and just smile, instead of going on, just smile and say, "not going there." Anya, she's really a sweet, gentle soul, says, "Shhhh. Just be quiet, don't spend your energies." They will work the energies, and heal, but do put flowers in there, too...in the bedroom. Your bedroom needs to be open to lots of light, especially in the next six months. Because your third eye is changing. You get cold, frigid feeling. They're opening something and it's overwhelming you right now.

You feel that your intuitiveness isn't working. Right now, it's not. When there is nothing, it's because you're looking too hard, and the energies are changing. You get disheartened with your spirit work, because you have a goal in your mind. Why? You don't need one. You need daily living. When you do that, all of a sudden, things will start to come in. So, no more goal setting.

Go to a belief system. Goals are for the earth; they are not for spirit. Spiritual development is from openness and when you set goals, then you lose the vision.

Your mother says, "I scrunched up far more than you realized." Because she would scrunch up her eyes' and see. She says, "You might try it, it works!" You know how sometimes you need that to focus differently. You think, "What am I doing?" Now, you can chuckle and say, "OK, Mom, I got it."

One of your dogs is not well. He is hurting. You need to get him checked. Animals work with vibrations. One ear is the trouble – there is a blockage. You can't leave it, because he'll lose part of his hearing, if he hasn't already. You can't afford to let that go. He has had trouble with his teeth. Poor little one. He's not having a good time. Attend to him, immediately.

Did you know you have a joy child? What were you doing around eleven years old? Did you play many hiding games, hiding under special something like forts or lean-to? Sometimes you'd get cold and shiver. This joy child was with you, then. It's a he. When you feel a tickle at the back of your neck, it's him...his name is Gus. He's cute as a button. He says, "I'm proud. I've known you for years, and now finally, I get to speak." He says he came into your life around eleven. You needed some uplifting around that time, from eleven to thirteen; it was a rather difficult time for you. (Author's note: My younger brother, Richard, passed away when he was ten years old, and I was eleven years old at the time.)

Spirit brought him in, and you got through it, quicker than you thought you would. Because by age thirteen, you were better again. You've never suffered from your brother's passing. You missed your brother, but you know he's okay. And it's true - he's fine. He and your mom are having a hoot over there. Just a real good time. You have to talk to Gus, sometimes. He says, "I was assigned to you at that point, because of those difficulties. When we were playing hide and seek, we were always one of the last ones to be found, we did well, didn't we?"

He says, "I really enjoy it when you eat chocolate. I can't taste it, but I get the feel of the energy. Just give yourself a little at a time, and keep it in the freezer, so that it melts when you put it in your mouth. If you do that, I'll work with you." He's a good guy, he's very proud. I like him. He says he worked with your brother also. Your mother had a hard time. She went into withdrawal for a while after he passed. She didn't get very much support from your dad at the time - interesting.

Your dad...there's some sort of regret going on with him. He does have some unfinished business with his family...a sister. She is hard to reach. She's an alcoholic. It hurts your father because she's the baby and he's the oldest. He never talks about it because this has troubled him. Light a candle to release that pain for him. Somewhere, he feels that he failed in being her brother, but he didn't. Cause she's a determined woman, a very different-natured woman from him.

You get into his energies, and talk to him about it. Talk to him about his sister. Somehow, you light a candle the night before you do this, so that you're connected with spirit, so that he finally releases something, I see him in tears. This is important, because this is hurting this man, and it's not his fault. His dad was always there, but not. It seems there was a duality with his father, so maybe his father walked two pathways. Nevertheless, there was a lot of onus put on your father. He should understand that there are rewards on the other side for this. When he crosses, he'll go with a smile. He's going to very gently walk out and go.

He sees his grandsons, his great-grandsons. You need to bring your grandsons to see him a couple of times more - they need to connect. Does he like the little one? If you can get one more visit in, it would be good. That little one has a cute giggle, from inside, just bubbles up. If it works out, it works out. Those two are somehow connected, and your dad will work with him (Christopher), when he passes. He will really be there for him.

End of transmission.

SOUL AWAKENING

I am Dancing Soul
I have danced through time
And space
And around the edges
Of souls who could not
Would not
Let me in
And I have also danced
To the music of the Universe
And with souls who knew
My dance
Because
The ecstasy
And lightness
Of the dance
Reminded them
Of home
And sometimes even
Awakened
A sleeping heart.

Gwen Randall-Young

CHAPTER 26

Accepting Responsibility

October 2001

I had been dating this one person off and on for almost two years. Most of his work occurred during the winter months, when he hauled stuff up north during the "winter roads" season. I do not like the long, cold winters of Winnipeg and could not wait to retire so that I could go live somewhere down South for the winter months. I could see that this would never happen if I continued this relationship. In addition, he loved his winter job and although he was quite a bit older than I was, he wanted to keep working his mid-seventies.

We had a lot of fun dating, taking dancing lessons, and attending Wine-makers monthly meetings and dinners. He was very knowledgeable on a wide variety of topics. He had a huge sailboat that he took out for weekends on Lake Winnipeg. I am definitely not into sailing, petrified as I was of water over 5 ft. deep, and so that was not doing to work either.

However, the most important thing that made me break it off with him was that he was an atheist and I was a spiritualist. I believed in healing through energy and exploring all other forms of healing. We were definitely not compatible on the most important level for me…and so, I decided to terminate the relationship completely, as sporadic interim dating was not working out for either of us.

This was in October, I could see the Christmas holidays approaching, and I felt I needed to make a complete break now, even if it meant spending the holidays alone. I made peace with myself over that and decided that it would not be a big deal to attend functions alone or with other family members.

It is difficult to end a relationship that does not serve you in the higher sense. You cannot be with someone who cannot express love, is always guarded, and does not believe in a higher power. If it goes against everything you believe in, listen to your body. It is telling you what the relationship is doing to you. I was constantly exhausted, always needing to sleep, kept having headaches and a sore stomach…those are all signs. I had to let go of that toxic (to me) relationship immediately.

What made it difficult is that he was a really, really, nice man…just not meant for me. It is important not to compromise, and to do what is right for your "self."

I had come to learn from my girlfriend Leslie the meaning of a mysterious dream that had haunted me. This woman of knowledge held the key that would open the gateway to my new circle of learning for me. Her explanations are in italics.

In this dream,

- There was a flood (You are experiencing an overflow of unconscious feelings. Your body is not involved. It is a purging, a renewal, and a new phase of life coming up for you.)
- Then, a tidal wave (finding your own way, emotions out of control.)
- The elevator crashed, rolled and stopped at kindergarten class (child with spiritual potential, alone, not hurt, not asking for help to get me out of here...not scared, no one else hurt, sore all over).
- Elevator going down (abrupt descent in to the un-conscious. Descent in search of new ideas and inspiration. Disappointment as you see a decline of your personal power and status. Part of you that needs re-assurance and security. Losing your place. Lack of confidence in own ability. The end of one cycle, beginning another cycle with renewed personal growth).

Armed with that knowledge, I knew that I had to face the fear of being alone, again. I accepted the dark nights of the fall and winter with grace and openness. I had learned that what you resist persists.

Sometimes, it is difficult to accept that certain situations arise in our life for a purpose and that we have something to learn from them. Some of the obstacles that women encounter, especially, seem so unfair... and they are! For example, there still are many double standards operative in the world of business and elsewhere.

What works for men often does not work for women in the same situation. This is not fair…true…and we resent it – as well we should. However, while we work towards trying to change the situation, it is important to see what we have to learn from these unfair obstacles and move on. We do not like them and it is up to us what we do with them.

Simply remember that no situation in itself is "negative." It just is. It is our perception of the situation that lends it either negative or positive energy. Sometimes, a situation that you thought was negative turns out to be a positive, later on when you review the same situation, looking at it from the big picture.

For instance, I always thought that leaving my husband, after 28 years of marriage, was a bad thing. In looking back, however, I see that my leaving freed me to explore new possibilities, which led me to a spiritual awakening and a totally new path – a path I could never have envisioned taking had I remained in that marriage.

It really is up to each of us to decide what we do with our lives. Never give up your decision-making power to anyone. There are events in the passage of our lives that elicit feelings we never knew were there and of which we believed we were completely incapable. Many of us have experienced the bitterness of having been lied to, cheated on, battered, beaten, molested, incested, spoiled, or over-indulged. All of us have feelings and memories we need to work through. None of us had perfect families.

The question then is how these experiences have affected us, and what we need to do to learn from our experiences. How do we work through those life lessons, integrate them into our being, turn them over, and move on. I always believe that the intensity of the whack on the side of the head that life has to give us in order to get a lesson through to us is directly proportionate to the height and breadth of our stubbornness and our illusion of control.

Life situations give us the opportunity to learn something new about ourselves. If we do not get the learning the first time around, we get another chance...and another...and another. If we miss the learning completely the first time, the next whack will be a little harder, and then the next time even harder. We get many opportunities to learn the lessons we need to learn in this lifetime, sometimes in the next, or in the next after that!

Can we look in the mirror and say to the person we see, "You are someone I trust and really admire?" We must remember that each step along the road of life is like taking a walk. It gets you somewhere, and steps often leave footprints. What you do becomes who you are. You are working with precious elements here. What you become is the price you paid for getting what you thought you wanted.

Looking back and regretting are very different from taking stock, making amends, and moving on. When we look back and regret, we are indulging in the self-centered activity of beating ourselves up over the mistakes of our past. All of us have made mistakes. We have neglected ourselves. We have neglected those we love.

Let's admit our wrongs and make amends to those we have wronged - including amends to ourselves when we have not been caring for ourselves. Let's move on. We cannot build on shame, guilt, or regret. We can only wallow in them, but owning and making amends for our mistakes affords us the opportunity to build on the past and integrate what we've learned into our future.

Once we recognize that all situations (good or bad, happy or sad) are gifts for learning, and we never really know what we have learned until we have learned it, then we are ready for the next learning. That's when we finally "get it."

Someone once said to me that if my life resembled a garbage dump, then it was up to me to sort it through, turn over the soil and plant flowers to make use of all the natural fertilizer...sort of a new twist on "if life hands you lemons, make lemonade."

Knowing Yourself

Know who you are.
Know who you aren't.
Know what you want.
Know who you wish to be.
Know what you already have.
Choose wisely from what you have.
Use faith and vision for your thoughts,
words and actions for best results.
Believe in the best outcome, for the good of all
Love and thank God for all you have.

Author Unknown

CHAPTER 27

Choosing Wisely

December 2001

The Christmas season was approaching and there I was - alone again.

I was doing a lot of office work at night on my home computer. One night, in early December, in the middle of a business email, I got a pop-up that was blinking "Match.com." I deleted it and continued working, when up it popped again. Again, I deleted it. My girlfriend Maureen had met her husband Joe through match.com a few years earlier and she had been prodding me to join Match.com. I kept resisting. When it popped up a third time, I paid attention. This time, remembering that when things come at you three times...pay attention, I stopped what I was doing and logged onto the match.com site.

I remembered what the psychic Erika had told me in September 1998 ..."You've got luck...good luck...good surprise.

Late luck, long life. I see a wedding ring, successful long marriage...no big compromises will be needed. Many trips with your partner. Tight on money at first, no problems later. Many trips together. Look out for yourself, though.

Pick a special day for you, for your wedding. Do not take any formal pictures before wedding. Feb-May when you'll meet. Lucky. You'll buy rings and set them aside. Good future. He has lots of love and a big heart. He is stubborn but trustworthy. He is not cheap...gives too much. There will be a wedding ceremony. He wants to marry you. Offers himself and his love. Good income, good foundation."

I also remembered what the spiritual intuitive Margaret had told me in August 1999: "...You're not destined to be alone. I see you with a very gentle soul, but not now - much later. He's not on your pathway for a while. However, the experiences lead you to a good understanding, you need grounding, but you need someone who can appreciate your energy field. You can keep a man young; you have that ability...to keep someone young. This man seems to be older, but you bring him younger. What you share together is very special. It's what you share with him... he just opens up your vision to a different kind of beauty and peace, but it's down the path, you don't know him yet."

Therefore, I told myself: "Well, it's now been a year and a half since that reading, and I must be getting close to the time when I will meet this person. Therefore, if I'm going to meet him through this method, I'll check out the site. After checking it out, I decided to enroll for one-month period. First thing I knew, I had written my profile and submitted a picture for approval. I paid the fifty-three dollar monthly fee. I told the universe that a month was plenty of time if this was the way I was going to meet him. If not, then after the month was over, I would look at another way of meeting this person.

I wrote my profile as follows:

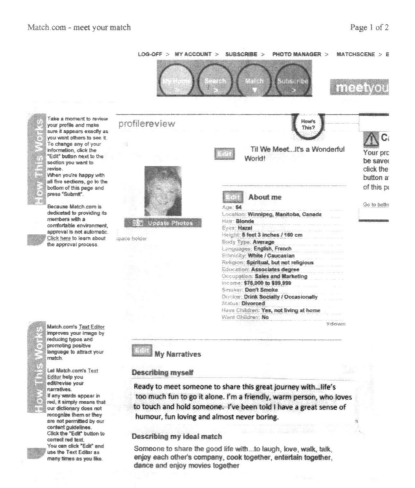

About My Personality

My ideal place to live is: Beach house

When it comes to my space: It's not perfect, but close

My fashion sense can best be described as: Sartorial - You're about luxury and quality and aren't afraid to show it off

My sense of humor tends toward: Light-hearted – I like cheerful, gentle fun

When it comes to parties I'd best be described as: Social butterfly

With free time on a day off, I would most enjoy: Curling up with a good book

When it comes to television: Opt for a movie

When it comes to work: I keep a standard 40-hour work week

I attend religious services: Rarely

My political views lean toward: Very Liberal

When it comes to money: I spend some, save some

When I'm meeting a friend, I am generally: Right on time

My favorite types of music are: R&B, Blues, Latin, Classical

Let's talk pets:

I have: Dog(s), Bird(s)

I like but don't have: Cat(s), Fish

I don't have and don't like: Reptile(s), Exotic pet(s), Rodent(s), Fleas

Turn Ons!	Turn Offs!
Skinny Dipping, Flirting, Public Displays of Affection, Dancing, Power, Money, Sarcasm, Brainiacs, Boldness / Assertiveness, Erotica	Body Piercing(s)

▼down

 About my match

Age Range Between: **50 and 60**

Location: **50 miles from R2N 3W9**

Hair: **Any**

Eyes: **Any**

Height: **From 3 feet 3 inches To 8 feet 2 inches**
From 100 cm To 250 cm

Body Type: **Slim / Slender, Average, Athletic, A few extra pounds**

Languages: **Any**

Ethnicity: **White / Caucasian**

Religion: **Any**

Education: **Any**

Occupation: **Any**

Income: **$50,000 to $74,999, $75,000 to $99,999, $100,000 to $149,999, $150,000+**

Smoker: **Don't Smoke**

Drinker: **Any**

Status: **Any**

Have Children: **Any**

Want Children: **No**

up.a

Privacy Preferences:

Your profile is currently: hidden

   ○ I want to show my profile

   ◉ I want to hide my profile

Well, when you pay for the services at match.com, they do the search for you, and e-mail you possible matches. I reviewed the rules with Maureen...

#1 never give your full name and/or address

#2 never give your home or business phone numbers

#3 always meet in daytime, at a very public place

Then, I sat back and waited. The first contact that I received was from a man in Minneapolis, Minnesota, which is 500 miles away...an eight-hour drive, in the USA. (Long-distance relationships very rarely work out...strike one). His name was John (my ex-husband's name was John...strike two). He had a beard on his photo (I believe that anyone with beards are hiding something...strike three). He was out – just like that.

The second possible match that I received was from someone living in Winnipeg. He was a math teacher at a local high school. He was a chess instructor and played in chess tournaments. (Okay, he has to be intelligent). Therefore, I emailed him back that we should meet for coffee somewhere, in the daytime (being careful not to give full name, address, and meeting at a very public, safe location). We agreed to meet for coffee, on a Saturday morning at Starbuck's Coffee Shop.

To be extra careful, I had my girlfriend Suzanne walking on the sidewalk outside, and I made sure I sat at a table by the window, so that she could see me at all times. He was late, came in and recognized me from the description I gave him...look for someone with blond hair, and wearing a red jacket. He was 6'4" (very tall), slim and good looking. (I'm only 5'1", so I'll get a pain in the neck every time I look up at him...strike one). I looked into his eyes, and saw nothing there (strike two).

We had coffee and talked for a while. It turned out that he had been divorced for 10 months (hmmm...too soon to start a new relationship...strike three). He was very bitter about it. We get to talking, and he told me about how he came to be divorced. He said, "...after 18 years, she just up and walked out on me. So, now I'm looking for someone to be with. I'm lonely. I hate cooking and cleaning for myself." (I was starting to get the idea.) However, I let him go on and on and on.

Then, when he finally asked a little about me, I answered that I was very spiritual, and that I'm a Reiki Master, and that I've learned so many lessons from my divorce, 7 years previous.

Then, I asked him, "Well, what do you think you contributed to the downfall of your marriage, what have you learned from your divorce, and what would you do differently next time?"

He replied, "I didn't do anything to contribute to the downfall of our marriage, and I wouldn't do anything different next time around. Learn? There's something I should learn?"

I reminded him gently, "Look, you've been divorced for only 10 months. You've started searching for a new mate for the last few months already. You haven't given yourself the time you need to grieve the end of your marriage, to analyze yourself and see where you went wrong and what you did right. If you do the work now, you'll get into the next relationship without repeating the same mistakes over and over until you finally get it."

Therefore, he said to me, "Well, that's why I need someone

like you in my life. I need someone to take me by the hand, and guide me to what I need to do and not do."

Meanwhile, I was thinking to myself, "No... I don't think so!" So, I took his hand and said, "No... This is something that you need to do for yourself. Please don't rush this process. Give yourself time alone, to get to know yourself first. Once you've healed yourself, then you'll be ready to find someone compatible with your lifestyle.

"You need to do some healing and figure out what lessons you need to learn from your previous relationship before jumping into a new relationship with someone else, otherwise you're bound to repeat the same mistakes. If you do the same thing today as you did yesterday, you can't expect a different tomorrow. If you circumvent this process, you'll wind up doing the same mistakes all over again, and you don't want that for yourself or for anyone that comes into your life."

Therefore, to sum it up, I looked him straight in the eyes and reiterated what I had been saying for the last hour, "Well, I think you're not ready for a relationship quite yet. However, I wish you all the best. Good luck and goodbye." And off I went to meet Suzanne, standing outside, waiting for me. She said she could tell right away from the look on my face, that this was not the one. I couldn't agree more.

The next day, I received an email from him thanking me for my honesty, and that upon reflection; he could see that he had, in fact, contributed to the downfall of his marriage. He said, "I really would like to see you again, as I can tell that I can learn a lot from you, and you can guide me through the process that I need to go through in order to get on with my life."

I replied, "No, thank you. I've just spent the last seven years going through that process for myself, and I think you need to do this for yourself, perhaps with professional guidance, if you feel you need it. God bless and good-bye."

Reflecting on this episode with my girlfriend Suzanne, I told her I could see the progress that I had made, that I actually said "no" to someone needy. That was a "wow" moment for me, and so felt strong enough to continue the search for a lifelong companion.

The third man that I met was a widower, whose wife had passed away two years earlier, of cancer. They had lived in Brandon and after her death, he had moved to Winnipeg to start a new life. Although two years had gone by since his wife had passed, he was nowhere near ready for any relationship. He was still grieving, and his lip quivered just in talking about her. (You don't want to start a relationship with someone until they have finished healing from the past one...otherwise, you'll end up being on the sideline in the new relationship until they have finished grieving, and working out the lessons they needed to learn from that episode in their life. That was not what I was asking the Universe to send me...so, not for me...strike one).

I really liked him. He was a very good-looking man, very nice manners. He was smart, and funny. We had a lot in common and I really enjoyed meeting him. However, there were no sparks between us (strike two). He was just a very nice person that one could have as a friend, but we both chose not to go that route (strike three). We said it had been nice to meet each other, wished each other good luck, good health and find happiness ...don't settle for anything less.

My bodyguard Suzanne was again standing outside, this one took almost two hours...so we decided that the next time; we would give each other a signal within five minutes. If he looked suspicious to her, she would let me know and, if so, she would come in and act surprised to see me there and just sit down with us and rescue me. On the other hand, if I felt that, it was safe for her to leave me; I would give her "the sign."

Usually, I believe in the power of three. This was the third one and no go. So now, what was I to do? I decided to continue my quest, as I still had over two weeks left of my month's subscription to Match.com.

The fourth person that I met, at the end of the second week, was a professor from the University. He was in his early fifties and had never married (oh...oh... maybe unable to commit? Strike one). He was very funny and smart, (but Omigod...immature! Strike two). He said, "Oh yeah, I've been on Match.com for over two years. It's a great way to meet women – at least he didn't say chicks."

I was intrigued as to why he had never married. While we were drinking our coffee, he replied, "Well, I've had a great time, travelled everywhere with usually one or two of my male friends but, now they're all married and the people who used to travel with me has dwindled down to none. So, I want to find someone who wants to travel with me and who has money to travel."

Then, he continued: "I've really enjoyed my bachelorhood, traveled all over the world. I've gone on many trips with man friends, girlfriends, but now, they're all settling down. I guess it's time I settled down too. (And here's the kicker)...After all, I'm not getting any younger. I have no kids and, I'm the youngest in the family, a good 10 years younger than my siblings are. So, it's time to grow up and bite the bullet." (Wow! I thought to myself, "Is that a statement that will bring women running?" Yes...but away from, not towards you...strike three). You're out!

"Plus," he continued, "I'm going to need someone to take care of me when I get older." Sarcastically, I replied, "I'm sure that you could pay a housekeeper or nurse for a lot cheaper than it's going to cost you to keep a wife." I thought to myself, "What a turn-off."

We had a great time and spent two hours talking about his life experiences and travels. He was a very interesting man. Although he had a great sense of humor and, made me laugh as he recounted some of his incredible travel stories, I could sense some-one who had never really grown up. He was fun to talk to as an acquaintance, as a friend, perhaps ...but as a potential mate for life...not for me, thank you.

I walked away with a sense of relief and a shake of the head. It turned out that one of my friends had gone to school with him, I found out later and that he was immature and narcissistic 30 years ago. Apparently, he was adopted by an older couple, was their only child and they just doted on him. He was their center of their universe, could do no wrong, and was denied nothing. Maybe that's what he chose for his lesson in this lifetime -to retain a childlike attitude and behavior. Oh well…it was not up to me a judgment, so move on!

After I got home, I called Suzanne and filled her in on the details of that meeting. We just laughed at how amazing life is, comparing the personalities and attitudes of all the different people that we have met over the years.

The question now was what strategy to use for the next person…#5? By now, I was feeling quite confident in the precautions that I was taking to meeting someone, so we agreed the next one I would handle by myself, but that I would phone her as soon as I got home.

I would never go directly home after leaving the crowded coffee shop, which was either Starbucks' or Tim Horton's coffee shops. I felt the safest there, a few miles away from where I lived, very close to a busy shopping mall. After leaving the coffee shop, sometimes, I would leave the car where I had parked it and walk over to the mall for at least an hour.

Then, I'd walk back to the car by a different entrance and drive over to a big apartment block, to visit a friend, or I would go to the library and read for a while. I would vary the routine…one cannot be cautious enough. This may seem silly but if you're thinking of meeting with people that you don't know, extreme caution makes sense.

A few nights later, it was getting close to the end of the month, when I got an email from "Venus from Match.com." The email stated that she had found someone who was 88% compatible with me and, that I should contact him directly. She included the direct link to his profile.

Now, if you look at a numerology book[6], the number five indicates a "person of action, the doer"...correlates to the letter "E." This letter represents someone with great analytical skill, the ability to understand and structure. It represents someone who is very stable and balanced spiritually, mentally, emotionally and physically.

The behaviors of a number five is: "having an active, clever mind, displaying mental curiosity; living an active life filled with versatility and variety; loving progress and personal freedom; embracing life's activities with a sense of adventure and being a great companion and fellow traveler.

I thought to myself, "Alright, then...this is more like it. This is the kind of person that I want to attract." None of the others I had met so far had a high compatibility rate... 88% compatibility really got my attention.

Well, I had not been the one to contact anyone yet and, where had that gotten me so far? With sweating palms and a pounding heart, I clicked on the link to his profile, and this is what I found:

---

6 Elinwood, Ellae. *The Everything Numerology Book,* Adams Media Corporation, Avon, Massachusetts, 2003., pp. 49, 59, 70, 102.

LOG-OFF > MY ACCOUNT > SUBSCRIBE > PHOTO MANAGER > MATCHSCENE

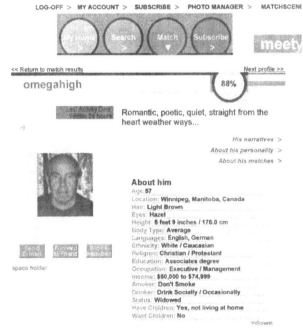

<< Return to match results

Next profile >>

omegahigh

88%

> My Matches
> My Profile
> My Photos
> My Account
> My Venus
> Profile Tips

> Email this person
> Send this profile to a friend
> Block this person's email/profile

To make contact, all you have to do is subscribe.

Match.com has engineered over a hundred marriages and thousands of meaningful relationships. Browse our latest success story.

Romantic, poetic, quiet, straight from the heart weather ways...

His narratives >
About his personality >
About his matches >

About him

Age: **57**
Location: **Winnipeg, Manitoba, Canada**
Hair: **Light Brown**
Eyes: **Hazel**
Height: **5 feet 9 inches / 175.0 cm**
Body Type: **Average**
Languages: **English, German**
Ethnicity: **White / Caucasian**
Religion: **Christian / Protestant**
Education: **Associates degree**
Occupation: **Executive / Management**
Income: **$50,000 to $74,999**
Smoker: **Don't Smoke**
Drinker: **Drink Socially / Occasionally**
Status: **Widowed**
Have Children: **Yes, not living at home**
Want Children: **No**

▾down

space holder

How he describes himself

A good conversationist in most topics. Kind with a strong sense of justice and fair play, and willing to give anyone a fair shake. In the younger days very athletic playing most team sports and now athletic retired to the golf course, and curling. Tactful, diplomatic and have a keen sense of humor. By nature peaceable and loving and will resent an injustice committed. In business marvelous at keeping my employees and associates happy. My instinct is for compromise and adjustment. In courtship I wield charm as a weapon. I hate to hurt anyone's feelings. I have a definite affinity toward women that dress well, not expensive but wear clothes that suit them. I like women with long hair, and moist lips. I enjoy quiet walks in scenic areas. Love out of place eatery's. Enjoy going to the movies or rentals at home. Dancing and quiet dinners. Love going to sport events such as baseball, football, or hockey. Enjoy shopping with a woman and picking out clothes for her. Sex for me is a rounded experience, not merely a quick tumble between the sheets. Love reading and writing poetry.

▾down

How he describes his ideal match.

A loving sharing person who will also be a best friend. Self centred, and dignified. Impetuous, unpredictable, alluring. Someone with emotions on the surface, and not hidden. Someone who smiles and has a fine sense of humor. Someone creative, daring, resourceful, and adventurous. Someone where routine bores her. Someone that yearns towards romantic places.

▼down

About his personality

My most ideal place to live is: Cabin in the mountains
When it comes to my space: Always clean for company
My fashion sense can best be described as: Contemporary - You're not about fashion awards, but not a slob either
My sense of humor tends toward: Light-hearted -- I like cheerful, gentle fun
When it comes to parties, I'd best be described as: Impartial Observer
With free time on a day off, I would most enjoy: Lunch with a friend
When it comes to television, I: Opt for the arts (A&E, Bravo, PBS)
When it comes to work: I keep a standard 40-hour work week
I attend religious services: Once a Month
My political views lean toward: Liberal
When it comes to money, I: spend some, save some
When I'm meeting a friend, I am generally: Right on time
My favorite types of music are: Alternative, Rock, R&B, Folk, Blues, Classical
Lets talk pets.
   I have: I'll tell you later
   I like but don't have: Cat(s), Dog(s), Fish, Reptile(s), Bird(s), Exotic pet(s), Rodent(s), Fleas
   I don't have and don't like:

Turn Ons	Turn Offs
LongHair	Tattoo(s), Body Piercing(s), Sarcasm

▼down

About his matches

Age Range Between: 48 and 58
Location: within 1000 miles of Winnipeg, Manitoba, Canada
Hair: Any, Auburn / Red, Black, Light Brown, Dark Brown, Blonde, Salt and pepper gray, White or gray, Other, Dark Blonde
Eyes: Any, Blue, Brown, Gray, Green, Hazel, Black
Height: From 5 feet 0 inches To 5 feet 8 inches
From 153.0 cm To 173.0 cm
Body Type: Average
Languages: English
Ethnicity: White / Caucasian
Religion: Christian / Catholic, Christian / Protestant, Christian - Other, Christian / LDS, Spiritual, but not religious
Education: Any, High school, Some college, Associates degree, Bachelors degree, Graduate degree, PhD / Post Doctoral
Occupation: Any, Executive / Management, Administrative / Secretarial, Finance, Political / Government, Artistic / Musical / Writer, Sales and Marketing, Technical / Science / Engineering, Teacher / Professor, Food Services, Legal, Medical / Dental, Labor / Construction, Transportation, Self Employed, Student, Retired, Other
Income: Any, $25,000 to $34,999, $35,000 to $49,999, $50,000 to $74,999, $75,000 to $99,999, $100,000 to $149,999, $150,000+, Less Than $24,999
Smoker: Any, Don't Smoke, Smoke Socially, Smoke Daily
Drinker: Any, Don't Drink, Drink Socially / Occasionally, Drink Regularly, Drinks

Well, needless to say, I was intrigued. I decided to email him. I did not keep a copy of that email, but if memory serves me right,

I told him just a few things about myself, and gave him the link to my profile and said if he was interested, to email me back. This was on December 29, 2001. My computer had a breakdown and I had to get it fixed, so did not get it back until January 12, 2002.

When I checked my emails, yes…there was a reply from #5. I found it ironic that we had both been away from our computers for close to two weeks. This was during the Christmas holidays, and so it hadn't bothered me not to have access to a computer. I felt I needed a good rest away from everything – computers included.

Anyway, here's his reply (private and personal information has been whited out):

```
Save Address(es)  Block
    From : Arvin
      To : estelle
    Date : Thu, 10 Jan 2002 01:40:38 -0800 (PST)
  Reply   Reply All   Forward   Delete   Put in Folder...

Hi Estelle
     Got your Email but could not see your profile so
don't know where you may be from...I just got back
from Alberta attending a wedding and went immediately
to work in Northern Manitoba so have been away from my
computer for a week...I work at an airport in Northern
Manitoba having a government contract and have 5
employees working for me...I stay two weeks and then
take two weeks off every month and spend most of it in
Winnipeg Manitoba but also do a lot of
travelling...Taking three weeks to go to Miami and
Orlando end of February to break up the winter...I
have no travel companions...Up here I stay in a cabin
on a river and snowshoe to the postoffice for the mail
and cross country ski on the river and wood
trails...In the summer canoe and fish up here and golf
in Winnipeg...Too soon to retire so will maintain this
life style...I have two sons living in Winnipeg of
which one is married and have 2 grandchildren...I was
married for 37 years until my wife suddenly passed
away two days before Christmas 2000 so have been in a
deep depression for a while but now looking to get on
and see whats in the future...You can email me at
                              as alot of
wilddogs and wolves around here...Any questions you
may have be free to ask...Well visiting hours are over
and must get back to work...Thanks for listening and
hope to hear from you soon...
Arvin
```

I replied with a little bit more history about my background, both personal and professional and myself. I'm sorry I didn't keep a copy of the exact wording, but it must have been enough information, as we continued to email back and forth over the next two weeks, and then this email came through from him:

Save Address(es) | Block |

From : Arvin

To : estelle

Subject :

Date : Fri, 25 Jan 2002 14:06:56 -0800 (PST)

Reply | Reply All | Forward | Delete | Put in Folder... ▾ |

```
Hi Estelle

I just got back from Norway house and the temperature
hit -40 the last three nights and froze the pipes in
the cabin so I wouldn't have minded the mosquito's
buzzing around...At least I could have used the
bathroom...Oh well will have two weeks in Winnipeg
before I go back to the frozen north...When was it you
were going to take me for coffee?...
Arvin
```

Well, this is it, I told myself. I'm going to meet him in person, finally!

If it's meant to be, he will be the one. Trying not to get my hopes up too much, I emailed him back on Wednesday, Jan. 30 (I didn't want to appear too eager or desperate.)

```
--- estelle Rose                              wrote:
> Well, I'll buy you coffee....when you come to
> Winnipeg!  When is that???
> Sorry to hear about the frozen pipes...that would
> not be fun!  I can't even
> imagine what you're going through.  I'm not a winter
> person...so it sounds
> like hell to me!  Looking forward to all your
> experiences "up north".
> Estelle
>
```

He replied:

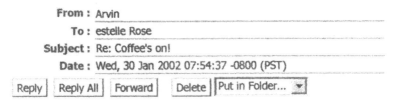

From :	Arvin
To :	estelle Rose
Subject :	Re: Coffee's on!
Date :	Wed, 30 Jan 2002 07:54:37 -0800 (PST)

Reply | Reply All | Forward | Delete | Put in Folder... ▼

```
Hi Estelle

Gosh I guess my communication is not that great as I
have been in Winnipeg for a week now and going back to
Norway House on the 5th of February for 19
days...Hopefully the pipes will have been thawed out
by then but things move pretty slow in the north...
   Coffee sounds great and I'm available anytime
except sat and sun when grandkids have my time
booked...
   Hope to hear from you before my return to the
frozen north...
```

He had included his phone number in the email but it still took me a few days to shore up my courage to give him a call, which I finally did on Friday afternoon. We agreed to meet on Sunday night at 7:00 pm at Tim Horton's Coffee Shop. I would be wearing a short white fur coat (as it was about -20 C. (-08 F.) that night. He told me he would be wearing a grey mid-length jacket.

I had never met anyone at night before, so this was a first. I was very nervous and parked really close to the entrance. From where I was parked, I could look into the coffee shop but I couldn't see anyone with a grey jacket.

Darn it, I was going to have to go in first!

"Oh well," I shrugged to myself, as it was very cold that night, "I'll just get a cup of coffee and enjoy my time alone until he shows up." I walked inside. There were only a few people having coffee and no one was sitting alone, wearing a grey jacket.

I stood in the line-up to get my coffee and when it was my turn, I ordered a coffee latte. As I pulled out my wallet to pay, a man passed in front of me and said to the server, "I'll pay for this lady's coffee and I'll have the same."

I was stunned and could only see his back. Then, I noticed he was wearing a grey jacket.

As he turned around and looked at me, I looked him in the eyes, and my knees almost buckled. I recognized him on a soul level (I swear to you).

I said to myself, "Oh my God...it's him. This is the man I've been waiting for. All this in the space of the time that I was looking at him and not saying anything.

He held out a cup of coffee and said, "Hi, I'm Arvin. You must be Estelle."

Just to make sure I wasn't projecting my own fantasies onto him, I looked into his beautiful hazel-green eyes, looked deep into his eyes - and I definitely recognized his soul.

"Yes, Omigod…it's Him. He does exist. He's here." I thought to myself, with my mouth still open and nothing coming out.

"Oh, great." I thought. "I've been stuck dumb. I can't speak."

Then, finally, my voice croaked out, "Hello, Arvin. It's so nice to meet you at last."

Love of family,

Love of life,

Love of self.

That I write so much on love must mean

that it is paramount to me.

This is for me a new beginning.

The end.

Estelle Reder

Addendum

Ten Steps to Spiritual Assistance and Awareness

Nine Principles of Manifestation

Eight Steps to Personal Change

Seven Major Chakras

The Six Laws of Harmlessness

The Five Reiki Principles

Four Affirmations

The Power of Three

Two Great Prayers

One House Purification Ceremony

Emotional Sources of Disease

Recommended Reading List

Testimonials

Love Them Anyway

About the Author

Afterword

That's My Story – Book 2

Seminars by Estelle Rose Reder

TEN STEPS TO SPIRITUAL ASSISTANCE AND AWARENESS

1. Enter into the Stillness…First thing in the morning: Meditate, just keep still, and when thoughts come into your mind, just accept and release them without judgment. Ask the for Godhead[7] for three things[8]:
    - Be very specific (give details…shape, color, size) as detailed as you can see it in your mind.
    - When asking for financial assistance, use abundance of financial energy (spirit understands abundance and energy, doesn't understand money and value of money).
    - Write it down (that way when you get it, you'll remember you asked for it).
    - End your request by saying: "This, I ask, for the good and benefit of all."

2. A Pact to Creating Your Day[9]…I'm taking this time to create my day and I'm affecting the quantum field. Show me a sign that you paid attention to any one of these things that I create today. Bring them to me in a way that I won't expect, so that I'm surprised at my ability to be able to attract these things. Make it so that I have no doubt that it's come from you. Thank you.

---

[7] Godhead = Father God, Mother Azna, or Universal Energy…whatever you are comfortable with, it doesn't matter what you call it, it is the intent that counts.

[8] Be careful what you ask for…make sure that what you ask for is what you really, really want…cause you may get it.

[9] Quote from the movie "What the Bleep do we know?"

3. Pay attention to déjà vu moments…they are an indication that you are on the right pathway for this lifetime. Notice what you are doing…and savor the moment.

4. Stay away from negative people…they suck your energy. If you need to be in their presence, protect yourself first by surrounding yourself with white light. Ask: "Universal Energy, surround me with your white light of protection," as you start, with your right hand, touch the bottom of your left foot, go counter clockwise to the top of your head and back on the right side, three times…making three circles around your aura/body.

5. Ask yourself what do you really, really want to be doing…this minute, this day, this job…, and then do it! Give yourself permission to be doing the things that you really want to do, instead of doing out of duty or obligation the things that you keep doing, with resentment (whether conscious or unconscious). Your attitude totally affects your experience.

6. Some illnesses are tied to your cell memory. Say this prayer: "Father God, Mother Azna (or Universal Energy), to any negativity that is resident in my cell memory, whether from this lifetime or a previous lifetime, whether conscious or unconscious; I demand that you leave imme-diately, with love, and find your way to the white light. I ask that this negativity within me, in the form of this disease or illness, be replaced with healing white light energy."

7. Ask and you shall be given. You don't ask...you don't get. Don't be afraid to ask the Universe for what you want. Say: " Father God, Mother Azna (or Universal Energy), my Guardian Angel, and all my spirit guides, this day and always, I ask for your guidance, assistance, love and protection, for the good and benefit of all."

8. You make the decision, and take the first step...no one else can do it for you...no knight in shining armor will come to your rescue. Once you have started the momentum going, help will come to assist and support you, at the right time, in the right place.

9. No action in life is in vain. Every relationship teaches you something. There are no rights or wrong, unless you don't learn from them. Each path will bring its own rewards. Ask not to have the experience, but accept help to get you through the rough ones. Bloom where you're planted!

10. The Blessings of Gratitude and Acknowledgment. Before falling asleep, every night, say this prayer: "Father God, Mother Azna, I thank you for all the blessings that have been showered upon me this day." Find the blessings that you experienced this day; review them and what you have learned from them; give thanks again, and release them in light and love to the Godhead.

Nine Principles of Manifestation[10]

1. Live from Your Highest Self

   "I have a divine ability to manifest and attract all that I need and desire."

2. Learn to Trust Your Divine Inner Wisdom

   "I trust in myself and in the wisdom that created me."

3. Honor Your Worthiness to Receive

   "I deserve to experience divine abundance, for I am a part of God."

4. Realize that You are Not Separate from Your Environment

   "I am one with my surroundings, aware of the connective energy between me and my world."

5. Attract to Yourself What You Desire

   "The divine creative power within me brings to me all that I want with happiness, love, and peace."

6. Connect to Your Divinity with Unconditional Love

   "I express the energy of unconditional love to all people and all things in my life."

7. Detach from the Outcome

   "I trust in the universal intelligence that created me to bring my desires to me in just the right way at the perfect time."

---

[10] Dyer, Dr. Wayne W. *The Secrets to Manifesting Your Destiny*. Nightingale Conant audiocassette Program.

8. Acknowledge Your Results with Gratitude and Generosity

   "I am deeply thankful for all that I have received, and I enjoy giving to others in the spirit of love and service."

9. Meditate to the Sound of Creation

   "I meditate each day to increase my awareness of the divine power within me. Through meditation, I am able to realize the beauty, grace, and love that directs my life and fulfills my deepest desires."

EIGHT STEPS TO PERSONAL CHANGE

- Take good long looks around you, and focus your attention on the beauty that surrounds you.

- Look for and find the many positive aspects of your life. Make promises sparingly and keep them faithfully.

- Have a forgiving view of people. Believe that most people are doing the best they can. Refuse to talk negatively about others. Instead, find opportunities to compliment or give encouragement.

- Letting go and surrendering to what is leads to peace, contentment, and joy. Love is found through acceptance, which begins within.

- Accept yourself exactly as you are right now. Know that you are okay and doing the best you can do right now. Let your virtues speak for themselves. Don't brag about your accomplishments.

- Know that what you have thought, said and done up to this point is enough. You are now more ready and able to do more, using this perspective. Keep an open mind.

- Decide to be more conscious, in the present, accepting and heart-full.

- Decide to take care of yourself with greater attention to your health and your happiness.

- By changing your attitude about life and focusing on peacefulness and acceptance, you will open yourself to manifesting miracles, through your thoughts, your attitude, and your gratitude.

The results are divine!

SEVEN MAJOR CHAKRAS

SEVENTH OR CROWN CHAKRA (Purple)

Spiritual Center

SIXTH OR THIRD EYE CHAKRA (Indigo)

Understanding, Imagination & Intuition

FIFTH OR THROAT CHAKRA (Sky Blue)

Power, Enthusiasm & Expression

FOURTH OR HEART CHAKRA (Green)

Love, Forgiveness, Healing & Peace

THIRD OR SOLAR PLEXIS CHAKRA (Yellow)

Wisdom and Knowledge

SECOND OR NAVAL CHAKRA (Orange)

Universal Order, Balance, & Creativity

FIRST OR BASE CHAKRA (Red)

Life, Strength & Survival

THE SIX LAWS OF HARMLESSNESS[11]

A state of harmlessness is based on Intent, moving through the Third Chakra. It requires one to take full conscious responsibility for every thought that one has, every action that one takes, and every other being that one interacts with. This full conscious responsibility also includes all soul-related interactions, whether conscious or unconscious, whether from this lifetime or any previous lifetimes.

The Law of Honor
Honor yourself and all other life forms.

The Law of Peace and the Law of Harmony
Unconditional acceptance of yourself and others.

The Law of Compassion
Unconditional love in action towards everyone and everything.

The Law of Divine Union
Correct the imbalance between masculine and feminine within.

The Law of Abundance
Release all material and emotional attachments
To achieve a complete balance between giving and receiving.

---

[11] Reprinted from the Library of New Age on-line Australia: Http://www.newage.com. "The Six Laws of Harmlessness", becoming the Bodhisattva, by Lord and Lady Rize.

The Law of Forgiveness

Allow all karma to be released by understanding the soul lessons.

Summary

Take conscious responsibility for your own personal spiritual evolution.

Blessings upon your joyous journey.

Namaste.

PRINCIPLES
Just for today
 do not worry
Just for today
 do not anger

Honor your parents
 teachers and elders
Earn your living honestly
Show gratitude to
 every living thing

靈
気

The Usui System of Natural Healing

FOUR AFFIRMATIONS[12]

For an Abundant and Blessed Life
I love you, God, and You Love Me.
    (Praises God.)

Thank You, God.
(List blessings God gave today.)
God, I attract your Blessings.
(Health, wealth, happiness, wisdom.)
God Bless and I Love…
(Bless family and friends, also
anyone you don't like.)

────────
[12] Reprinted from Paul McManus, Creator of Prayer Power CD's.

The Power of Three

Things happen in 3's…pay attention. There is no such thing as a coincidence. However, things do happen for a reason. The universe is guiding you towards a certain path, person, or thing.

In the morning, light a white candle. Ask the Universe for three things today, be very specific. It's okay to ask for money…ask for the abundance of financial energy…the universe understands abundance and energy.

Test three places when you want to ask for something. Be careful what you ask for – you might get it! To make sure you are asking for the right things; check it if feels right mentally, in your head – what is your brain thinking? Check in your heart – what is it feeling? Check with the stomach – what does your gut tell you? If all three are okay…proceed with your request. If one of them is telling you no…stop and think it out before going ahead.

After you have asked for three things, always finish your request with "for the good and benefit of one and all." If your request fulfilled would wind up hurting someone, or changing you to become greedy, or mean…then, you don't want it, right? "What matters if you've conquered the world, if you've lost your soul in the attempt"?

This lifetime will go by quickly; but your soul will go on infinitely. Think about it. By living consciously, being in the moment, in the "now," you will start recognizing opportunities that present themselves to you. If an idea or the thought of someone comes to your mind once, pay attention. Twice, take notice; and three times…do something about it. The universe is sending you a message, take action!

Another time when the power of three comes into play is when you are going into a job interview. Ahead of time, prepare notes on paper for yourself, under the heading:

Three strong points; three weak points; and the reasons why I want to work for this company. For example, three strong points:

- Highly organized
- Very positive attitude
- Self-motivated

Three weak points: This is a trick question! Only give one: for example, "Well, I'm not crazy about paperwork, but I'm very conscientious about deadlines and getting it done. Other than that, I can't think of any other." Leave it at that. Don't say any more. Shut up. Let them ask the questions. Most often, interviewers don't want your life history; they want short brief answers.

I have interviewed hundreds of people. Most often, the people who didn't get the jobs were the ones that rambled on and on, not shutting up. "If I hire this person, they will talk the ears off anyone who will listen and waste valuable time." So, turn the mouth on low and keep it under control.

Give three reasons why you would want to work for this Company. For example, you could research the company ahead of time and say, "Well, I've read your annual report and I'm impressed with: your growth year after year, the many opportunities available to employees, and the innovative five-year plan report." Then, shut up. Do not give any more details or information, unless they ask. Be specific and be brief.

Two Great Prayers

1. Morning and Evening Prayer

I love you, God.

Thank you, God, for loving me.

I give thanks to you, God, for you are good.

Your love endures forever.

I love you because you loved me first.

I love you, Lord my God,

With all my heart, mind, body and soul.

My God loves.

The earth is full of his unfailing love.

I follow your command:

Love each other.

I love my neighbor, as I love myself.

I do not seek revenge,

Or bear a grudge against any of God's people.

I love all people,

Animals & plants of the earth.

God, you are inside me.

In your wisdom,

You give me strength.

You give me love.

You give me happiness.

You attract blessings to yourself and me.

I am healthy, happy, and wealthy.
I am happily married.
I have a great family and wonderful friends.
Send me your guidance,
Assistance, love, and protection,

2. A PRAYER TO A SLEEPING CHILD[13]

Move close enough to your sleeping child that he or she can hear your quiet voice without being awakened by it, and then say some version of the following, in whatever words come easily from your heart

"My dear child:

I feel blessed that you chose me as the caretaker and nurturer of your sacred spirit as it starts its new life on earth.

I promise you with the best effort of my soul to keep you safe, healthy, and happy. I promise to help keep you connected to the God who created you and who lives inside you with every breath you take.

May you keep all the joy and wisdom your past lives has given you, and may all sorrow, fear, illness, and negativity from those past lives be released and dissolved for all time into the white light of the Holy Spirit."

The spirit you're talking to through the subconscious is ageless and as fluent as you are. The peace, security and healing you can give your child during sleep really will make a difference, not only to them but also to the bond between your divine spirit and theirs.

---

[13] From Sylvia Brown's "The Other Side and Back"

ONE HOUSE PURIFICATION CEREMONY

Ingredients: salt, a white candle, and holy water.

Salt is an ancient symbol of purification, and the white candle simply represents positive spiritual energy.

To make holy water, simply let ordinary tap water sit in direct sunlight for three hours, and three times during those three hours, make any sign over it that has spiritual meaning and power for you. (One example would be the sign of the cross.)

Starting at night, on the stroke of a third, or Trinity, hour – 3:00, 6:00, 9:00 or 12:00, light your way with the white candle and spread the salt around the outside of your house until it's completely encircled.

Pause at each of the doors and windows and sprinkle them with holy water, again making the sign of your faith or carrying its symbol.

Once you've finished enclosing your house in a circle of salt and sealed its openings with holy water, move inside and go from room to room, still carrying the white candle.

Bless every room with more holy water and the sign of your faith or its symbol, and keep repeating the same prayer from one end of the house to the other:

Beloved Father and Mother God…cleanse and purify this room with the white light of the Holy Spirit. Purge all negativity from within and fill it with your Loving grace."

Amen.

EMOTIONAL SOURCES OF DISEASE

Problem	Source
Accidents	Expressions of Anger, frustration, rebellion.
Anorexia/Bulimia	Self-hate, denial of life, nourishment, "not good enough."
Arms	Ability to embrace, old emotions held in joints.
Arthritis	Pattern of criticism of self and others, perfectionism.
Asthma	Smother-love, guilt complex, inferiority complex.
Back	Upper: not feeling supported emotionally, needing support. Middle: guilt. Lower: burnout, worrying about money.
Breasts	Mothering, over-mothering a person or thing, place or experience. Breast cancer: deep resentment attached to over-mothering.
Burns Boils, Bulimia	Anger. Anger. Anger.
Sores, Swellings	Anger. Anger. Anger.
Cancer	Deep resentment, distrust, self-pity, hopelessness, helplessness.

Colon	Constipation is inability to let go, diarrhea is fear of holding, constipation = lack of trust of having enough, hoarding.
Ears	Too hard to accept what is said. Earaches = anger. Deafness = refusal to listen.
Feet	Self-understanding, moving forward.
Fingers	Index = ego, anger and fear. Thumb = worry. Middle = anger, right: a man; left: a woman. (Hold with other hand to release). Ring = unions and grief. Little = family and pretending.
Genitals	Femininity or masculinity issues, rejecting sexuality: "Sex is dirty," "women's bodies are unclean." Bladder infections: being pissed off, Holding in hurts. Vaginitis: romantically hurt by a partner. Prostate: self-worth and sexual prowess. Impotence: fear or spite against mate Frigidity: fear, sexual guilt, self-disgust. PMS: denial of female cycles or female worth. VD: sexual guilt.

Hands	Holding on too tightly to money or relationships. Arthritis = self-criticism, internalizing criticism, criticizing others.
Head	us, what we show the world, something radically wrong.
Headaches	Invalidating the self.
Heart	Heart is love and blood is joy. Heart attacks are a denial and squeezing out of love and joy.
Knees	Inflexibility, unable to bend, pride, ego, and fear of change and stubbornness, self-righteousness.
Legs	Fear or reluctance of moving forward, not wanting to move. Varicose veins = standing where we hate.
Lungs	Inability to take in and give out life, denial of life. Emphysema or too much smoking = denial of life, Inferiority.
Migraines	Anger and perfectionism, frustration. (Masturbate to stop)
Neck	Flexibility issues.
Overweight	Needing protection, insecurity.
Pain	Guilt seeking punishment. (Notice where it manifests.)
Sinus	Irritated by someone.

Skin	Threatened individuality, others have power over you. Thin-skinned, feeling skinned alive, need Self-nurturing.
Stiffness	Stiff body = stiff mind, inflexibility, fear, "Only one way", resistance to change. (Where it manifests = where pattern is.)
Stomach	Inability to digest ideas and experiences. Who or what can't you stomach? Fear.
Strokes	Negative thinking, stopping of joy, Forcing change or direction.
Swelling	Stagnated thinking, bottled-up tears, Feeling trapped.
Throat	Fear of change, inability to speak up, anger, Frustrated creativity. Sore Throat or Laryngitis = too angry to speak. Tonsillitis or Thyroid = stifled creativity, Leukemia = deeply stifled creativity
Tumors	False growth, tormenting an old hurt, not allowing healing. Uterine tumors: nursing
Ulcers	Fear, not being good enough, lack of self-worth.

RECOMMENDED READING LIST

Anderson, George and Barone, Andrew. Walking in the Garden of Souls. New York, NY: G. P. Putnam's Sons, 2001

Anderson, Joan Wester. The Power of Miracles. The Ballantine Publishing Group, 1998

Ball, Pamela. 10,000 Dreams Interpreted. Arcturus Publishing Limited, 1997

Bowman, Catherine. Crystal Awareness. St. Paul, Minnesota: Llewellyn Publications, 2003

Breathnach, Sarah Ban. Simple Abundance: a Day book of Comfort and Joy, Warner Books, Inc., 1995

_____ Something More: Excavating Your Authentic Self. Warner Books, Inc., 1998

Dyer, Dr. Wayne W. The Secrets to Manifesting Your Destiny, Nightingale Conant Corporation, 1996

Eadie, Betty J. Embraced by the Light. Placerville, California: Gold Leaf Press, 1994

—- The Awakening Heart. New York, NY: Simon & Schuster, Inc., 1996

Hanh, Thich Nhat. The Heart of the Buddha's Teaching. Berkeley, CA: Parallax Press, 1998

Kabat-Zinn, Jon. Wherever you go, There you are. New York, NY: Hyperion Publishers, 1994

Kowalski, Gary. The Souls of Animals. Walpole, NH: Stillpoint Publishing, 1991

Myss, Caroline. Anatomy of the Spirit. New York, NY: Three River Press Publishers, 1996

Redfield, James. The Celestine Prophecy. New York, NY: Warner Books, Inc., 1994

_____ The Tenth Insight. New York, NY: Warner Books, Inc., 1996

Schoen, Allen M. Kindred Spirits...How the Remarkable Bond between Humans and Animals can Change the Way we Live.

Sedlacek, Dr. Keith. Finding the Calm Within You. New York, NY: McGraw-Hill Publishing Company, 1989

Selby, John. Kundalini Awakening...A Gentle Guide to Chakra Activation and Spiritual Growth. New York, NY: Bantam Books, 1992

TESTIMONIALS

These are only a few of the many testimonials given to Estelle Reder for her healing work in private spiritual consultations and seminars.

Dear Estelle:

I am so sorry we had to run out on your wonderful hospitality. You are an impressive host. What a great workshop. I love all of the handouts. You are such a testament to what you are sharing. You look great and you exude good energy. Thanks again for setting that up for us. Please make sure to include my email on your next workshop invitation.

Helene Bulger,
Winnipeg, Manitoba
October 29, 2007

Hi Estelle,

I had a Reiki healing session with you before returning to Regina after a visit to Winnipeg. You did Reiki Surgery on my stomach, where I had been experiencing a lot of pain (an exorcism - so to speak). Whatever was inside was removed (the pain did not return) and my drive home was most enjoyable. I would say that you targeted the demons and sent them packing in a very short time. Impressive, Estelle! Although you are new to this "job," you are obviously destined for bigger things.

Thanks my friend!

Leslie,
Regina, Saskatchewan
October 2003

Estelle,

I just finished reading your book – fabulous! I couldn't put it down. Absolutely fascinating! This has to be an all time record for me for reading a book! I am not a fast reader but it pulled me in and would not let me be until the very end. Great ending, by the way. Just perfect! I LOVED IT! I am so glad you wrote it and so glad you finished it. It's way more personal than I anticipated but a lot of the personal stuff is what makes it interesting. I loved the way you incorporated Reiki and your spiritual growth and insights into it. It really works and, I think, will make it a keeper for people. I loved the pics! I loved the Master symbols, the match.com screen captures, and the poems at the beginning of every chapter. There were so many wonderful extras! Moreover, the addenda were really good. You did such a great job! Wow, Estelle! What a super book! Ok, where's Book 2? I want to read more and I'm sure your readers will want more. You did good! Thank you so much for letting me read it and entrusting your only copy to my care!

Marianne Gillis
Winnipeg, Manitoba
December 19, 2008

Hi Estelle,

I hope things are going well. I want to thank for teaching me Reiki, Levels 1 and 2. My mom passed away on Feb 17 and I am so glad I knew Reiki. I used the healing energy with her and my brothers and sisters as well as for myself. She had the most peaceful, beautiful transition anyone could hope for. Thanks again for sharing your knowledge...

I have been doing Reiki on myself whenever my knees are sore. Most times, I felt so good after that I did not need to take an aspirin...what does it all mean. Reiki works!

Marie-Claire
Winnipeg, Manitoba
January 20, 2009

Estelle,

For me I found you to be a very charming, intuitive, and captivating mentor. I took the course, "Manifesting Your Desires" on November 15, 2008. I found it had a tremendous effect on my approach to life. After the course,   I found myself not wanting things so badly and starting to "Take the time to smell the roses." I began to feel more at ease and my confidence level built up. I've learned through your teachings that we are all equipped with the abilities we need to become what we want to be. The key is to "Believe" in ourselves and get rid of all the doubts that prevent us from getting what we want out of life. We need to implement "Affirmations" and know that the universe has an enough abundance to supply humankind with all of its needs.

Shirley
Winnipeg, Manitoba
November 20, 2008

Dear Estelle,

Your seminar "Manifesting Your Desires" was simply awesome. You're among the nicest people I have ever known. Thank you for the positive healing messages and the new enlightenment you have given me. Your kindness and generosity is overwhelming. The handouts and all the free stuff you gave away at your seminar were fantastic. Lots of information given and supported by your own personal stories...overall, a great experience. Thanks for everything.

Susan
Winnipeg, MB.
November 2008

Dear Estelle,

I remember one day going to your house for a visit. When you answered the door, I just burst into tears. I had no control whatsoever, which freaked me right out as I always had to be in control, due to the job I had. I was apologizing like crazy and embarrassed beyond words, even though deep down inside, I knew you would find it okay. Later on that afternoon, you suggested doing a Reiki healing session. Not knowing what would take place, we started the session. I fell asleep soon into the session until your hands reached my heart. I felt myself welling up and my throat had a lump so big in it I could hardly swallow. As you moved your hands towards my throat, I burst into tears. I could not believe that I actually cried for at least 3 hours. I kept apologizing, and you kept saying it's fine - this happens. By the end of day, I could not believe how much lighter my heart was and how much better I felt after this Reiki session.

When I was a young girl, my mother used to blame me every day how I had made her sick. She had been diagnosed with Multiple Sclerosis when she was pregnant with me and hardly missed a day in reminding me in the meanest of ways. I felt nothing but pity and hatred for her. However, having said that, whenever I spoke of her, I would get teary eyed. I talked to you about this and you suggested that perhaps a Reiki Surgery session where you could cut the psychic cords still attached to my mother from me. This surgery was performed and I felt instant relief. I noticed that after the next few Reiki sessions, that I had tears still. We did another Reiki Surgery, to ensure that all the psychic cords had been cut. That last session must have worked because I can now talk about my mother in a detached way, with no tears and even more important - no hatred. Thank you so very much for all you continue to do.

Diane Harris,
Flin Flon, Manitoba
June 2008

Dear Estelle,

After a healing session with you, I feel reconnected, grounded, and at peace. It's the warm feeling I associate with Home. Thank you for the healing gift of Reiki.

Karen,
Lorette, Manitoba
Jan. 21, 2009

Dear Mom,

I've watched you get very knowledgeable, passionate, and a complete professional in this field. You are always looking out for people's best interests and ways of helping people. You emit positive energy at all times and people find you so very easy to talk to. You understand that there are many different ways of healing oneself and that each person has their own path to follow. You have gained so much knowledge through your numerous relationships – from your friends (male and female), from your personal life experiences (divorce, moving), from your professional dealings. You can speak about so many topics on so many levels....There is Mother Theresa...then there is MY MOM.

I LOVE YOU. I'm proud of you and honored to be your kid.

Marc Penner,
Winnipeg, Manitoba
February 5, 2009

LOVE THEM ANYWAY

People are unreasonable, illogical, and self-centered.

Love them anyway.

If you are kind, people may accuse you of selfish ulterior

motives.

Be kind anyway.

If you are successful, you will win some false friends and true

enemies.

Succeed anyway.

The good you do today will be forgotten tomorrow.

Do good anyway.

Honesty and frankness will make you vulnerable.

Be honest and frank anyway.

What you spend years building may be destroyed overnight.

Build anyway.

People need help, but may attack you if you try to help them.

Help them anyway.

In the final analysis, it is between you and God.

It was never between you and them anyway!

Mother Theresa

AFTERWORD

I am always interested in hearing from readers who would like to share their stories, angel encounters, miracles, answers to prayer and other heavenly wonders or situations in their life where mysterious workers have appeared with just the answer they were praying for.

Please email me at or visit my Website:

If I can use your story in any future reference work or in my seminars, I will contact you for permission.

Happiness keeps You Sweet,
Trials keep You Strong,
Sorrows keep You Human,
Failures keeps You Humble,
Success keeps You Glowing,
But Only God keeps You Going!

Estelle R. Reder

THAT'S MY STORY - BOOK 2

Moving Down a Courageous Path

Creating New Beginnings, Working with the Healing
Energies of Reiki, Chakras, Auras, Spirit Animals,
with guidance from an Ascended Master, a Swami,
and a Guruji.

Estelle R. Reder

Follow Estelle's journey, as she moves deeper into her spiritual
journey. Estelle follows her guided inspirations to develop and
offer seminars to help others in their journey.

Of those seminars, one student wrote: "What a great workshop. I love all of the handouts. You are such a testament to what
you are sharing. You look great and you exude good energy."

Another student wrote: "I found Estelle to be a very charming,
intuitive and captivating mentor. The course "Manifesting Your
Desires" had a tremendous effect on my approach to life - I found
myself not wanting things so badly.

A third student wrote: "I've learned through Estelle's teachings
that we are all equipped with the abilities we need to become

what we want to be – to believe in ourselves. We need to implement "Affirmations" and know that the universe has abundance to supply all of humanity's needs."

In Book 2, she will continue to share with you her personal stories – among them being an encounter with a Guruji, His Holiness Sri Sri Ravi Shankar, that inspired her onwards, an Ojibway aboriginal sweat lodge experience, and a channeling with Babaji, an Ascended Master.

SEMINARS BY ESTELLE ROSE REDER

Manifesting Your Desires Seminar

Create A Life of *Unlimited Abundance and Happiness.* What is the real meaning of success and abundance? Can we live a spiritual life in a material world? Can we have our heads in the clouds, with our feet on the ground? Can you become truly content, prosperous, and eliminate fear, anxiety and worry in every area of your life? Absolutely! Once You Know How.

Attracting Abundance and Happiness doesn't happen only if you're "Lucky", or one of the fortunate few or that it is only possible through sacrificing other important areas of life. Regardless of what you may have been taught and led to believe "You are a limitless being who exists in an infinite and limitless Universe with limitless potential to achieve anything that you can conceive in your mind". You Only Need "Awaken" To The Fact That It's True.

During this Seminar, I will share with you a wealth of life changing information and tools, these tools will restore your belief in your abilities to create for yourself, the life that you really want, filled with vibrant health, inner strength, and clarity of purpose.

How to Attract Love and Romance Seminar

Estelle Reder is a powerful advocate of personal empowerment. She shares compelling stories and insights, and the tools to live with integrity, peace, and balance. "Tap into a life of abundance"!

In this seminar, Estelle Reder will show you how to prepare yourself physically, mentally and spiritually to attract the ideal person into your life, or how to put back the love and romance into an existing relationship. She invites you to step out of your comfort zone and try something new. During the Seminar, you'll learn how to:

1. Prepare yourself physically through opening your heart and root chakras
2. Ask the Universe for what you Really, Really Want in an ideal soul mate.
3. Prepare your house and bedroom for love and romance, through Feng Shui
4. Attract the best person in your life, through meditation

Follow your inner voice—the quiet guidance of your Higher Self

NOTES

NOTES

NOTES

LaVergne, TN USA
31 August 2009
156549LV00002B/3/P

9 781608 602537